Jesus Gardens Me

DAVID JACKSON

A Follower of Jesus

Contents

Acknowledgements 5

Preface 7

Introduction 11

Section One: From Inspiration to Research to Theory.......... 16

1. Research Focusing on Jesus' Occupation 17

2. Cross Cultural Anthropology................................... 21

3. The Garden in the Bible and Beyond 27

4. "Fanciful Speculation" or "Fruitful Contemplation?" 41

Section Two: Jesus Gardens me... 58

5. Autobiographical Scan 59

6. Consciousness Raising Trips 65

7. Spiritual experiences 97

8. Additional Education from Travel, Music, and Art 105

9. My Reading Life.. 109

Section Three: Further Application For Life 116

10. May Jesus Garden You 117

Postscript 121

Notes 125

Bibliography 129

Acknowledgements.

BACK IN 1996, I SENT the biblical scholar, Dr. John Pilch, a brief article speculating on the occupation of Jesus. He has written a series of books on *The Cultural World of Jesus*. He advised me to "read my colleague, Doug Oakman, *Jesus and the Economic Questions of His Day*". Luckily, I found this book in the Library of the Catholic Theological Union in Chicago. (It is now out of print.)

A year later, I revised my article and re-sent it to Dr. Pilch, who responded: "After reading your previous paper, I was chatting about your paper with Doug Oakman at our annual meeting in Portland, Oregon. He shared his insights about the plausibility of Jesus being an itinerant worker."

Then a few years later I saw a reference to Oakman's more recent book *Jesus and the Peasants*, 2008, which I read with enthusiasm. Several of the chapters he had published previously in scholarly journals, but five were new. With his permission, I have quoted freely from these two books.

Indeed, his response to my seeking that permission was supportive: "Hello David. If my efforts help yours, then feel free to quote. John Pilch was a great friend. May your work grow a Garden of Eden for both of us!"

In 1996, I also sent the article mentioned above to Father Eugene A. LaVerdiere, S.S.S., a leading American Scripture scholar, from whom I had taken a course, Luke's Gospel, as part of my Master's Program at Catholic Theological Union. Fr. LaVerdiere wrote his encouraging comments and suggestions on the pages I had sent: "The trail is very interesting! Stay on it." His genuine humanity came through with these words: "Thank you for your letter and the investigation piece—Sherlock Holmes with his magnifying glass."

In seeking other permissions, I received further encouragement:

Fr. Peter Schineller, SJ wrote: "David—Peace--I sent you a note giving you permission -- as far as I can --to use the material from *Christ the Gardener.*" He went on to add "and here is more info-- and a very special etching by Albrecht Durer, *Christ the Gardener.*"

I asked Erin Lothes for permission to publish her eco-reflection, which she wrote on the web site "Catholic Women Preach", as a post-script to my book. She responded: "I would be pleased. Please send me the title and table of contents of your book so I get a sense of what you are doing! Many congratulations."

From friends I have received encouragement and affirmation. Maureen Conrad assisted in developing a personal approach to my travels. She got me in touch with Joe Burke who also made helpful suggestions. She introduced me to Barbara Nevers.

Barbara has been a Godsend to me in the publishing process. The debt of gratitude I owe to her is way beyond what I can express here. In a truly inspiring gift of generosity, she gave of her time to offer suggestions and to do careful, detailed, and accurate editing. If you find it readable, credit Barbara. I do.

The members of the intentional community to which I belong were encouraging and affirming.

Preface.

"Listening to the stories of fellow believers eager to share how God is working in their lives is positively painful, and recounting such narratives to others is embarrassing," notes theology professor Luke Timothy Johnson.*1 (Numbers in bold and italics refer to end notes.)*

This statement gives me pause. What I want in presenting how God is working in my life, is for the reader to find inspiration and growth. I begin (in section 1) by sharing how my research has helped me to meet Jesus again for the first time (to borrow a thought from the theologian Marcus J. Borg). Recounting this narrative has been inspiring and positive for me and I hope it will be so for you.

In Section 2, I reveal how I see that God has been working in my life in the past and now continues to do so.

The conviction that others can gain something from my experiences has been a guiding principle for me as it was for Johnson, who asks, "What, finally, should we hope for from such a sustained effort . . .?" He continues May Believers "listen attentively to the stories of the experience of God's activity in their own lives and the lives of others; they can embrace and celebrate . . . the distinctive mode of expressing how divine power is present within creation".

I share this hope.

Johnson expresses a second desire "We can hope that believers will view the signs and wonders in Scripture as invitations to perceive

God's presence and power in their own lives, and will view the signs and wonders in their own lives as an interpretive entry into understanding the signs and wonders of Scripture, for it is the same Living God at work in both."

I seek this same dynamic through sharing my own understanding of the signs and wonders of Scripture. For example, Mark 9:32-37 which begins with the Second Prediction of the Passion: "But they did not understand what he was saying and were afraid to ask him". Then they came to Capernaum; and when he was in the house, he asked them: "What were you arguing about on the way? But they were silent, for on the way they had argued with one another who was the greatest."

This episode reminded me of an experience I had, which I think is symbolic of many events in our lives. A priest who was a clinical pastoral supervisor at an institution for juvenile offenders was speaking to us, a group of theology students. Something he said prompted one of our professors to make a rather snide remark to those sitting next to him. Father John interrupted what he was explaining and asked, "Do you have a question?" A stunning silence followed.

Notice, that in the passage from scripture the disciples are afraid to question Jesus. We have similar experiences at times of being afraid to question. Jesus describes the conversation as "arguing" And again the disciples remain silent. A different translation of this passage has Mark, the narrator, describing the conversation as "discussing among themselves". When Mark tells us what they were talking about, we understand their silence "They had been discussing among themselves who was the greatest".

Have you ever had an experience of someone whispering a snide remark?

Have you ever been afraid to ask about something you did not understand?

Have you had the experience of describing an incident in one way and then hearing someone else describe it quite differently? For

instance, a conversation that you would consider a discussion, but another person might view as an argument.

In my last chapter, Section 3, I summarize Teresa of Avila's stages of prayer. She offers a process for us to ponder in building a renewed encounter with Jesus Christ.

My hope is that, assisted by some reflection questions, you will see Jesus as the Gardener at work in your life.

Introduction.

MY STORY WITH JESUS THE Gardener goes back many years. It was the Easter season and I was walking in the Boerner Botanical Gardens in Milwaukee, Wisconsin. It was early in the morning, and the appearances of Jesus as chronicled in the Gospels were dancing in my head. I had met a number of gardeners so it was natural that as in John 20, the appearance of Jesus to Mary Magdalene in the garden had come to mind. At first, she thought he was the gardener. I found myself asking, "What exactly did Jesus do for a living?" "He was a carpenter" was my answer. Then it occurred to me that maybe I should check out the Greek text that is the basis for that claim.

Later that day I walked into the library of Sacred Heart School of Theology to research that text. Upon entering, I met one of the librarians who said, "You sure are in a bouncy mood today." I jokingly responded "Well I was praying in the Garden at Whitnal Park. I thought I met Jesus, but it was only the gardener." As the words came out of my mouth, I suddenly found myself thinking, "What if Mary wasn't mistaken? What if the person she met after the Resurrection *was* Jesus the 'gardener'?"

My research took me to some interesting, inspiring, and new insights about Jesus. My searching revealed Scholarly interpretations, differences of interpretation, personal inspiration, prayerful reflections, artistic masterpieces, fruitful contemplation, and fanciful speculation. I felt that I was indeed meeting Jesus again for the first time.

Scholars, prayers, and artists have reflected on John 20. The following two posts are representative of the variety of interpretations: Victoria Emily Jones, writing on the blog, Christianity and the arts, "She mistook him for the gardener", offers seventeen artistic works presenting Jesus as a gardener.2 James David Audlin, arguing from Aramaic and Greek translations, titles his view: "No Mistake: Mary was Right to Think Jesus was the Gardener."3 After my initial questioning, "What if Mary wasn't mistaken? What if the person she met after the Resurrection was Jesus the 'gardener'"? My thoughts went in that direction. On the one hand it seemed they were farfetched, but on the other hand it had a certain feeling of charged inspiration.

After these initial ruminations, I looked up the Greek word for carpenter, *tekton.* This aroused my curiosity and led me to the *Concordance to the Greek New Testament* to learn how many times it was used. In addition, I wanted to discover how many times the Greek word for Gardener appeared in the New Testament. Only once, I discovered.

I also discovered that the only direct information given to us in the gospels about Jesus occupational pursuit is incidental and brief. Under "carpenter," there were only two citations. Matthew. 13:55 "Is not this the carpenter's son?" and Mark 6:3 *"Is not this carpenter, the son of Mary and brother of James and Joses and Judas and Simon, and are not his sisters here with us?"* A sudden rush of excitement came over me. I blurted out to no one in particular, "You mean that the entire tradition of Jesus as a carpenter rests on these two texts?" I discovered that actually it depends on one text, that of Mark. In Matthew, the question simply asks if Jesus is the *son of a Carpenter.* According to Matthew, Jesus may not have been a carpenter as his father was. The context of the passage, which names Jesus clearly as a carpenter, is embedded in the text, which speaks of Jesus' brother and sisters. Commentators have even noted that making him the son of a woman (Mary) may have been a put-down. If Jesus were the main support of a family of at least six younger children and a widowed mother, it would give further emphasis to the fact that he had to find work. Biblical scholar John Meier, in *A Marginal Jew,* states, "The size of the family would argue for both the need and the ability of his family unit to provide at least some of its food from farming"4 which was logical, as they lived close to the fertile slopes and fields of Lower Galilee. Further on Meier notes: "When Jesus forsook his clearly defined social role as the woodworker of Nazareth to assume the ambiguous role of itinerant teacher and wonderworker, he left an assured position of honor—however modest—to enter a position that meant high honor in the eyes of believers and great shame in the eyes of opponents."5

That great shame arose from Jesus moving away from the prevailing norms of honor and kinship. This movement was a process beginning when "In those days Jesus came from Nazareth of Galilee and was baptized by John in the Jordan" (Mark 1:9). As John "appeared in the wilderness" which was outside the established social system, in leaving his family and village to travel to a wilderness, he symbolically steps outside the kinship network in which he was born and raised.6 He leaves his assured position of honor.

Mark's Gospel goes on to tell of Jesus returning to Galilee after his baptism and beginning his ministry. He gathers disciples, heals, and teaches. I believe the great crowds now following him overwhelmed his family. Clearly, they must have heard something of the content of his preaching which was announcing something new and different from their traditional Judaic faith. However, I also believe they were afraid for his safety. Travel in antiquity was dangerous and indeed considered deviant behavior except for certain specified reasons (feasts, visiting family, certain kinds of business). For protection people travelled in groups. According to Mark, those who came to listen to John came in groups. Jesus' family came from Nazareth to Jerusalem for the feast of Passover when he was twelve years old. They were part of a group. Group travel was much safer. At this point in his life however Jesus' band of companions is just forming. According to Mark's chronology, the first disciples Jesus calls are four fishermen. He then goes on his way and calls Levi. Chapter 3 begins with the healing of A Man with a Withered Hand on the Sabbath after which we learn, "The Pharisees went out and immediately conspired with the Herodians against him, how to destroy him." 3:6. This early introduction of the plan to kill Jesus led Martin Kahler to make his famous summary: Mark's Gospel is a "passion narrative with an extended introduction".*7* Shortly after in this chronology Jesus goes up a mountain and appoints twelve that they might be with him. Then he comes home.

Gradually we see defined more clearly the stress that Jesus caused in the area of kinship. In chapter 3:20, 21" Then he went home and the crowd came together again, so that they could not even eat. 21 When his family heard it, they went out to restrain him, for people were saying, "He has gone out of his mind." 22 And the scribes who came down from Jerusalem said, "He has Beelzebul, and by the ruler of the demons he casts out demons." After Jesus experiences rejection at home and from the Jewish officials he begins his itinerant ministry in Galilee almost entirely in villages and the countryside among the peasants: farmers, fishers, artisans, and day laborers. "His activity involved a serious critique of the "powers that be," a fact that is central, not peripheral, to the tradition.*8* Jesus is departing from the Jewish tradition in which he was raised.

If I may engage in a bit of speculation: Commentators have written extensively on the question "Did Jesus actually have brothers and sisters?" Catholics have been at pains to say "no" the word can mean cousins. The next question that came to my mind was: "Could it be possible that this topic so dominated interpretation that people overlooked the question of Jesus' occupation?"

Victoria Emily Jones in her post, "She Mistook Him for the Gardener," has a wealth of artistic images on this subject. I discovered that "Jesus the Gardener was a traditional theme of orthodox scriptural exegesis and popular preaching whose origins can be traced back to patristic times. Pre-modern exegetes taught Mary's misidentification was a reminder of a spiritual reality: Jesus is the gardener of human souls. The same teaching continued to be spread in the fourteenth through eighteenth centuries in texts popular and considered authoritative."*9*

This history surprised and excited me. It also acquainted me with the expression "Jesus is the gardener of the human soul." Prior to discovering this material, I had come to the title of this book *Jesus Gardens Me*. My words are different, but I do identify with him as the gardener of my soul. It is a spiritual reality in my life. I explore this theme and share how I've seen it worked out in my life.

Section One:

From Inspiration to Research to Theory.

Chapter One
Research Focusing on Jesus' Occupation.

Continuing my research, I discovered that some manuscripts of Mark changed from directly stating "Jesus the carpenter" to the indirect wording of Matthew, the "son of a carpenter". The renowned Biblical Scholar, Raymond Brown, in an appendix in his book, *The Birth of the Messiah* quotes a 1955 article in the *Catholic Biblical Quarterly*. There the author states that the Greek word **tekton** covers a "wide range" of artisans in stone, wood, and (in Late Greek) metal. Some even interpreted the word to mean blacksmiths. Some took it to mean shipbuilder and architect.*10*

Speculation on the occupation of Jesus goes beyond the meaning of *tekton*. The *Infancy Gospel of Thomas* goes in a very different direction: "And again in seedtime the child went out with His father to sow corn in their land. And while His father was sowing, the child Jesus sowed one grain of corn. And when He had reaped it, and threshed it, He made a hundred kors; and calling all the poor of the village to the thresh-ing-floor, He gave them the corn, and Joseph took away what was left of the corn. And He was eight years old when He did this miracle."*11*

The biblical scholar Douglas Oakman writing in *Jesus and the Economic Questions of his Day* (1986), states: "It cannot be doubted, that most of the residents of the village (Nazareth) occupied themselves regularly with subsistence agriculture. Jesus came from peasant stock and without question was socialized early to the routines of farming."*12*

Clearly, the identification of Jesus' occupation seems to be more complicated than the simple tradition that identifies him as "carpenter." I discovered in The *Catholic Biblical Quarterly* the article that Raymond Brown refers to, an eleven-page detailed analysis of Woodworking Products, Tools, and Techniques, Materials, Socio-Economic Status, and finally a summary.*13* For me, however, the conclusion is established on the second page: "To call him a 'carpenter' is to use the word in a rather loose sense".

John Meier in his first volume of *A Marginal Jew* asks "Was Jesus a Poor Carpenter?" He concludes:

> Thus, while Jesus was in one sense a common Palestinian workman, he plied a trade that involved, for the ancient world, a fair level of technical skill. It also involved no little sweat and muscle power. The airy weakling often presented to us in pious paintings and Hollywood movies would hardly have survived the rigors of being Nazareth's *tekton* from his youth to his early thirties.

Meier also offers his view of the social stratification at the time of Jesus:

> Small farmers in particular led a precarious existence, sometimes at subsistence level, subject as they were to the vagaries of weather, market prices, inflation, grasping rulers, wars and heavy taxes (both civil and religious). Further down the ladder were day laborers, hired servants, traveling craftsmen, and dispossessed farmers forced into banditry. . . . At the bottom of the ladder stood the slaves, the worst lot falling to slaves engaged in agricultural labor on large estates—though this was not the most common pattern for Galilean agriculture.*14*

In a more recent Facebook post, Dr. James D. Tabor of the Department of Religious Studies at the University of North Carolina writes: "Whether he (Jesus) was a skilled day laborer, a contract worker or perhaps even a managing contractor, we have no way of knowing." **15**

A quick look at the development that takes place in the chronology of the four Gospels reveals something interesting. The predominant agreement places them as written in this order and these times: Mark, c. 70, Matthew, c. 80, Luke, c 80, and John, c. 90. However, notice what happens. In Mark Jesus is "the carpenter, the son of Mary and brother of James and Joses and Judas and Simon, and are not his sisters here with us?" In Matthew Jesus is the son of the carpenter. Luke phrased the question, "Is not this Joseph's son?" John, asks "Is not this Jesus, the son of Joseph, whose father and mother we know?" As time went on the Gospel writers distanced themselves from naming Jesus a carpenter. You will also notice that Mark identifies him in relation to his mother, and then the identification switches to the father. We can speculate as to why this development took place. Matthew, Luke, and John seem to be getting away from maternal identification, which was not the tradition: in addition, it may be a slur suggesting that Jesus is illegitimate.

In the preaching of Jesus, the parables clearly hold a dominant position. John R. Donahue, SJ, a renowned Scripture expert, even wrote a book titled *The Gospel in Parable*. In the preface, he writes ". . . the parables, like all great literary and artistic works, are ever old and ever new and resist capture by any one movement or period . . . For the past century the parables have served as the royal road to the *life, teaching, and self-understanding* of Jesus." **16** I wondered if they might also be a road to the "*occupation* "of Jesus.

It has struck me how dominant agricultural images are in the parables. This one, found only in Mark 4:26-29, is a good place to start. Jesus shows considerable knowledge of the process of growth in agrarian life:

26 He also said, "The kingdom of God is as if someone
would scatter seed on the ground, 27 and would sleep and

rise night and day, and the seed would sprout and grow, he does not know how. 28 The earth produces of itself, first the stalk, then the head, then the full grain in the head. 29 But when the grain is ripe, at once he goes in with his sickle, because the harvest has come."

My own study on the dominance of agricultural images in the parables produced these results: In Mark, the first of the synoptic Gospels, there are four parables and they all take their imagery from agriculture. Three of them also appear in Matthew and Luke. From the material particular to Matthew, five of ten are clearly agricultural. From the material that is particular to Luke, five of the fifteen parables are agricultural. (There is a move toward the cities in Luke.) We can summarize thus: fifteen of the thirty-five synoptic parables, or 43%, are agricultural. John, though not using the word "parable," uses agricultural imagery in abundance: "harvest . . . reaper . . . sower. . . . The Vine and the branches. . . . His Father is the vinedresser."

I have put emphasis on the life experiences of Jesus. He clearly was a careful observer of agrarian life. Oakman, however, is cautious when commenting on the agrarian parables which have long been considered to reflect the mores and experiences of the countryside." He raises this question: "Does this replay Jesus' own experiences? It is probable that they do at least in a typical sense."

Was Jesus just an observer of agriculture or is a different interpretation possible? To be sure, He was an itinerant preacher. However, is it possible that like Paul he also was an itinerant worker? Is it possible that the connection that the basic Christian communities make with Jesus as a fellow (*campesino*) *migrant farmer* are not just figurative but literal? Is it possible that Jesus is talking about himself and some of his experiences in some of his parables?

Chapter Two
Cross Cultural Anthropology.

At the time Jesus lived on this earth society was completely segregated along class and gender lines. So, when He is identified as a *tekton* what exactly is his social or economic class? Scholars propose various answers to this question. Borg seems to have a twostep process 1) "In terms of social standing a *tekton* was at the lower end of the peasant class who still owned a small piece of land. 2) We should not think of a *tekton*, as being a step up from a subsistence peasant farmer; rather, a *tekton* belonged to a family that had lost its land."*17* I believe Jesus' family went through these two stages.

The Biblical scholar Dominic Crossan makes this broad statement: ". . . in general the great divide in the Greco-Roman world was between those who had to work with their hands and those who did not."*18* The Roman Empire was an agrarian society. Living in this society, what might life have been like for Jesus?

There was an abysmal gulf separating the upper from the lower classes. Even in Jesus' time, one percent owned half of the land. Belonging to this class were rulers, governors, priests, military generals, and merchants. On the other side, the vast majority of the population were characterized as peasants, two thirds of whose annual crops went to support the upper classes. Their life was clearly one of insecurity. It cannot be doubted that most of the residents of a village like Nazareth occupied themselves regularly with subsistence agriculture.

Besides affirming that agriculture was such a dominant occupation in the Middle East, Professor Pilch elaborates further, " . . . Work had a figurative meaning in the minds of the ancients." He lists these examples "O my threshed and winnowed one, what I have heard from the Lord of hosts, the God of Israel, I announce to you." : Isa 21:10 "Jesus said to him, "No one who puts a hand to the plow and looks back is fit for the kingdom of God." Luke 9:62 "36 When he saw the crowds, he had compassion for them, because they were harassed and helpless, like sheep without a shepherd. 37 Then he said to his disciples, "The harvest is plentiful, but the laborers are few; 38 therefore ask the Lord of the harvest to send out laborers into his harvest." Matt 9:36-38, *19*

Oakman observes that most of the residents of Jesus' village, Nazareth, occupied themselves regularly with subsistence agriculture. Since Jesus was of Peasant stock without question, he was socialized early to the routines of farming. Oakman also cautions that there is no way of knowing more precisely, however, about the relationship between the pursuit of a craft and agriculture in these villages."*20*

Loss of land was a regular occurrence. A bad year meant disaster. Drought, debt, disease, or death forced occupants off their land and into share cropping, tenant farming or worse. Pilch offers another example of people losing their land. Scholars guess that since Joseph took Mary to Bethlehem to register for the census (Luke 2:4) but was himself an artisan living in Nazareth, at some earlier period in the family history Joseph's family probably lost ancestral land in Bethlehem."*21* The Biblical scholar, Jose A Pagola compiles a list, including parables and other teachings of Jesus to illustrate how Jesus shared the suffering of his people. Included in the list he writes ". . . his proclamation of blessedness for the indigent, the hungry, and those who weep over their lost land" is part of this list. It struck me that Pagola includes "their lost land" in what people wept over.*22*: ""Blessed are you who weep now, for you will laugh." Luke 6:21b What specifically is the cause of people weeping, Jesus does not say. Pagola believes loss of land was one cause of their weeping.

Cross-cultural anthropology puts the artisans in a class of people who came from those who lost their land. Below this class were the degraded and expendable. If Jesus was a carpenter he had been pushed into the dangerous space between peasants, degraded, and expendables. Oakman seems to me to describe a bit of his life experience. "If economic opportunities were scarce, or when the local peasantry had nothing left to pay the artisan, he could be expected to travel to where work was. As a rule, the craftsman of antiquity exported his labor power, rather than a product. Rural craftsmen like Jesus were probably under greater pressure to travel in order to find work than were artisans of great urban areas."*23*

Oakman ends this section on Jesus' occupation telling us that ancient carpenters in the Mediterranean frequently worked on boats. He gives a little more information on the call of the fishermen at the Lake of Galilee and considers the possibility that Jesus may have built the boats of his early disciples Peter and Andrew, James and John." *24* In writing about Jesus' social contacts Oakman states: "Jesus could easily have found employment related to the fishing industry. As he had to travel about somewhat to carry on his business, and as he possibly carried materials of his trade through toll points, he would have come to know the man in the toll collector's booth as well, It is likely that Jesus met these people prior to events recorded in the extant gospels."*25*

I believe Jesus' labor power included carpentry but also other types of work. Oakman quotes from the ancient Greek historian, Xenophon: "In small towns the same man makes couches, doors, ploughs and tables and often he even builds houses, and still he is thankful if only he can find enough work to support himself." Oakman comments: "This text attests to the 'jack-of-all-trades 'quality of rural carpentry—diversification compelled by economic necessity. The text also reveals the economic impulse that drove the ancient rural carpenter to seek work where it could be found."*26* In a later book, *Jesus and the Peasants,* Oakman further states, "Occupationally, Jesus is best understood as a peasant child forced to leave the village in search of livelihood."*27*

Biblical scholar John Meier in *A Marginal Jew* brings another dimension: "When Jesus forsook his clearly defined social role as the woodworker of Nazareth to assume the ambiguous role of itinerant teacher and wonderworker, he left an assured position of honor—however modest—to enter a position that meant high honor in the eyes of believers and great shame in the eyes of opponents."*28*

Many of the people Jesus associated with were poor. However, he also had contacts with wealthy people. "Many of the parables that evidence a detailed knowledge of large estates, the behavior of slaves and overseers, and so forth, undoubtedly derive from Jesus' direct experience with these situations. Clearly, the Gospel tradition is not equivocal in stating that Jesus ate with tax collectors and sinners. Around the meal, Jesus was able to bring together all of the constituencies—rich and poor—that he had built up in his many travels."*29*

My experience in the Rio Grande Valley of Texas has a bearing on this issue. So many Mexican immigrants are not limited to one type of labor. They are multi-talented "jacks of all trades." They are not limited to one category. The same person can be carpenter, electrician, mechanic, painter, gardener, and landscaper, and what is true of the multi-talented males is true of the multi-talented females.

One example of the implications of Jesus experience comes through in the prayer we know as the "Our Father," giving a different understanding to two petitions: "forgive us our debts "and "give us our daily bread." Taxation and debt crushed people. Oakman explains: "Therefore, rather than release from infractions against God, Jesus primarily asked through this petition for release from earthly shackles of indebtedness. The problem of debt, oppressing the people of Palestine and controlling their lives, is so vast that only God's power can effectively remove it."*30*

Oakman offers this proposed translation for "give us our daily bread": "give us today bread in abundance." The prayer is asking for release from the earthly shackles of indebtedness which threatens the availability of daily bread.

Toward the end of his book, Oakman makes several powerful (and probably controversial) statements. In the chapter "Jesus the Tax Resister he states "Jesus' historical activity was essentially about politics and the restructuring of society, and not about religion or theology. Jesus was a conservative in relation to the traditions of Israel." His contemporaries advocated violent resistance to Rome. Jesus did not. Oakman's final words in this chapter describe not only a past reality but also a present one: "While Jesus' historical resistance to imperial and colonial realities left its traces in his traditions, it is also true that the canonical gospels of the New Testament shifted Jesus' focus from social relations to relations between human beings and God. In this sense, the New Testament made an early contribution to obscuring the meaning of Jesus' resistance."*31*

Oakman captures another shift away from Jesus' message:

"... in time, or perhaps even during Jesus' own lifetime, the scribes of the Greek sayings of Jesus became sympathizers ... But what was originally in the Jesus movement a social critique of Herodian Galilee becomes in later written Jesus tradition an indictment of Judean political religion (critique of Pharisees, judgment against "this generation"). Ironically, in this understanding of developments, the words of the original indictment against Jesus are turned into His indictments of others. This transformation—from Jesus' religious politics in the interests of Galilean peasantry to the political religious contest between the nascent Christian movement and rabbinic Judaism (as we see in Mathew)—depended centrally upon a palimpsest Jesus, an illiterate peasant whose own interest were roughshod overwritten by those of the scribes of the kingdom.*32.*

The shift that Oakman discerns in the canonical gospels of the New Testament was further amplified when Christianity opted for the religion of empire under Constantine. "This was reflected not just in accommodation to the Roman Empire after Constantine, but through the spiritualization of Jesus' prophetic message. The combined influence of Greek philosophy and Roman imperial social structures shifted the emphasis from fostering egalitarian relationships and transforming the world to the goal of saving one's soul."*33* This quotation is found on the back cover of Wes Howard-Brook's book. Rather than Catholicism changing the empire, the empire changed Catholicism.

My Theory

Clearly, the Gospels present Jesus on the move. I believe that His family experienced some type of disaster, possibly the death of Joseph that forced them off their land. It might be that they had a bad crop and could not generate income. On the other hand, perhaps taxes, both civil and religious, overcame them. Something forced Jesus to "travel to where work was." I also believe that Jesus "exported his labor power, rather than a product." I believe this less glamorized picture more accurately describes His hidden life experience, as quite different from that of the happy holy family living in peace and contentment. Jesus lived among those who for one reason or another were forced into begging, prostitution, tax collection or other occupations not directly connected to working the land. It is important to remember the words of Marcus Borg who reminds us that *tekton* was at the lower end of the peasant class, and not a step up from a subsistence peasant farmer as we might view such skilled workers today: "So the Biblical scholar, Stegemann rightly says that the popular movement "associated with the name of Jesus was a movement **of the poor for the poor**".*34*

Jesus did not make an option for the poor, He lived poor, and out of this experience, He preached and attracted followers. In terms of the content of His preaching, I am convinced that Oakman is correct in his conclusion that Jesus' historical activity was essentially about politics and restructuring society. The New Testament began to obscure the meaning of Jesus' resistance. Religion and theology were not the dominant theme in his preaching. Rather its focus shifted from social relations to relations between human beings and God.*35*

Chapter Three

The Garden in the Bible and Beyond.

Easter Moment of Jesus and Mary Magdalene in the Garden Tomb Area.

FOLLOWING MY INSPIRATION, THEN RESEARCH and finally my theory, I return to expand my original experience of the Easter Moment of Jesus and Mary Magdalene in the garden tomb area. Only from John's Gospel do we learn about the burial in a Garden. Only in John's Gospel do we learn of Mary Magdalene's experience there—where she met Jesus and mistook him for the gardener, although whether Jesus did some gardening in his itinerant life remains an open question.

We begin, as in 19:41, 42 the garden assumes center stage: "41 Now there was a garden in the place where he was crucified, and in the garden, there was a new tomb in which no one had ever been laid. 42 And so, because it was the Jewish day of Preparation, and the tomb was nearby, they laid Jesus there."

In Chapter 20, the story of Mary Magdalene is continued: vs. 1, 2. "1 Early on the first day of the week, while it was still dark, Mary Magdalene came to the tomb and saw that the stone had been removed from the tomb. 2 So she ran and went to Simon Peter and the other disciple, the one whom Jesus loved, and said to them, "They have taken the Lord out of the tomb, and we do not know where they have laid him

Then, while Peter and John race to the tomb, Mary's story continues in vs. 11-18:

> 11 But Mary stood weeping outside the tomb. As she wept, she bent over to look into the tomb; 12 and she saw two angels in white, sitting where the body of Jesus had been lying, one at the head and the other at the feet. 13 They said to her, "Woman, why are you weeping?" She said to them, "They have taken away my Lord, and I do not know where they have laid him." 14 When she had said this, she turned around and saw Jesus standing there, but she did not know that it was Jesus. 15 Jesus said to her, "Woman, why are you weeping? Whom are you looking for?" Supposing him to be the gardener, she said to him, "Sir, if you have carried him away, tell me where you have laid him, and I will take him away." 16 Jesus said to her, "Mary!" She turned and said to him in Hebrew, "Rabbouni!" (which means Teacher). 17 Jesus said to her, "Do not hold on to me, because I have not yet ascended to the Father. But go to my brothers and say to them, 'I am ascending to my Father and your Father, to my God and your God.' "18 Mary Magdalene went and announced to the disciples, "I have seen the Lord"; and she told them that he had said these things to her.

Connection between God the Father and gardening

The Bible makes explicit the connection between God the Father and gardening: In Genesis 2:8 "And the LORD God planted a garden in Eden, in the east; and there he put the man whom he had formed". Thus, the world's first gardener was God. Other biblical books too have metaphors to continue the image as in the Hebrew Scriptures Isaiah 61:11: "For as the earth brings forth its shoots, and as a garden causes what is sown in it to spring up, so the Lord GOD will cause righteousness and praise to spring up before all the nations."

Moving into the New Testament, we find agricultural images in abundance and specifically about Jesus as a gardener, as in John 15, 1-5:

> 1 I am the true vine, and my Father is the vinegrower. 2 He removes every branch in me that bears no fruit. Every branch that bears fruit he prunes to make it bear more fruit. 3 You have already been cleansed by the word that I have spoken to you. 4 Abide in me as I abide in you. Just as the branch cannot bear fruit by itself unless it abides in the vine, neither can you unless you abide in me. 5 I am the vine, you are the branches. Those who abide in me and I in them bear much fruit, because apart from me you can do nothing. I am the true vine, and my Father is the vinegrower. He removes every branch in me that bears no fruit. Every branch that bears fruit he prunes to make it bear more fruit. You have already been cleansed by the word that I have spoken to you. Abide in me as I abide in you. Just as the branch cannot bear fruit by itself unless it abides in the vine, neither can you unless you abide in me. I am the vine; you are the branches. Those who abide in me and I in them bear much fruit, because apart from me you can do nothing.

John's Gospel goes further, as previously described (19:41 and 20:11-18), when Jesus and Mary meet at his tomb. This Gospel, in a variety of ways, explores the newness that comes with Jesus. Paul, in Romans 5:12–21 and 1 Corinthians 15:21–22, 45, speaks of Jesus as the second Adam. "These allusions suggest that Jesus is the gardener of the new Eden, doing what Adam could not do. His resurrection broke ground in this garden, marking the beginning of a massive restoration project."**36** Such biblical references suggest why so often we find Jesus toting a shovel in the resurrection art of Renaissance and Baroque Europe. He is the gardener of humanity, bending down to bring us up, to make us full, healthy, and beautiful.

The renowned preacher Charles Spurgeon, in a sermon on the topic back in 1882, declares: "Behold, the church is Christ's Eden, watered by the river of life, and so fertilized that all manner of fruits are brought forth unto God; and he, our second Adam, walks in this spiritual Eden to dress it and to keep it; and so by a type we see that we are right in 'supposing him to be the gardener.'" *37*

Many commentators have noted the striking parallels between the beginning of John's Gospel-- "In the beginning was the Word . . . . . ."-- and that of Genesis: "In the beginning, when God created the heavens and the earth . . . . "In the second chapter, Genesis tells us: "The Lord God planted a *garden* in Eden." Is the story of Mary Magdalene in the Garden a symbolic story of theological artistry or a historical reality? John uses variety to illustrate to us the new beginning happening with Jesus. I lean toward historical reality, but I found in my exploration that many people have preached on the story as symbolic theological artistry. (In later chapters, I will provide a number of examples of the latter, which have personally enriched me spiritually. I see them as Jesus Gardening me.)

Another aspect of the garden scene often explored is seen in the words of the Vulgate, Noli me tangere. (Touch me not.) Scholars go back to the Greek and Aramaic Texts.

1. One of the sources I explore is ACADEMIA. *(Academia.edu* is an American social networking website for academics. The platform can be used to share papers, monitor their impact, and follow research in a particular field.)

A frequent contributor to this web site is the biblical scholar James David Audlin who posted "No Mistake: Mary was Right to Think Jesus was the Gardener." He has translated the Gospel of John from Greek and Aramaic into English. Audlin's work has been characterized thus: "The common assumption is that in John 20:15 Mary is mistaken to think Jesus is the gardener. This brief essay suggests, by an analysis of the text and its cultural context that she wasn't as mistaken as all that." Mr. Audlin argues from Greek and Aramaic languages. Here is a sample:

> The common assumption is that the gospel author means in John 20:15 to explain Mary's subsequent statement by saying she mistakes Jesus for a gardener. Yet the text says nothing even to imply a mistaken identification, just that she 'supposes' or, in the Aramaic, hopes. In addition, the text says not 'a gardener' but 'the gardener', in both Greek (*o κηπουρος*, ho kēpouros) and Aramaic (ܓܢܢܐ ganānā). If anything, it should be read, as 'the Gardener' for this is not just any gardener. Remember that there has been garden imagery all along, from 19:41 back to 18:1, and to 15:1, wherein 'the gardener' is first mentioned, albeit with a synonym. **38**

Audlin goes on to ask who Mary hopes this is. There is a comparison to Adam in the Garden of Eden, but actually, there it is God not Adam who is The Gardener. Audlin also notes that Psalm 104 images God planting and caring for his people and states that Classic Near Eastern literature "is full of references to the God-King as gardener". He also goes back to John 15:1 where Jesus himself names the Gardener as God and. ends with this brief summary: "John the Presbyter's usual subtlety has Mary fail to recognize Jesus but still be right to identify this figure as (made in the image of) 'the Gardener."

2. The prominent biblical scholar Sandra Schneiders comments:

> . . . the translation of vs. 17 is usually translated as "Do not hold on to me," or "Do not cling to me". " . . . we should read, "Do not continue to touch me" or even more literally,

"Not me (emphatic) continue to touch . . . What Mary is told not to do is try to continue to touch Jesus, that is to encounter him as if he were the earthly Jesus reinstated. The time for that relationship is over . . . I would suggest that what Jesus is really doing is redirecting Mary's desire for union with himself from his physical or earthly body (which in any case does not exist because it is the glorified Lord who stands before her in an appearance which is temporary) to the new locus of his presence in the world, that is, the community of his brothers and sisters, the disciples.39

3.   Titian.

'Don't touch me', says Jesus to Mary Magdalene, recoiling. Mary has come to the grave that morning to embalm the body of Christ. To her amazement, Jesus is walking around alive. She first mistakes him for the gardener, which is why Titian has him holding a spade.

Irony has it that the crux of the story is presumably based on a translation error. The Greek source text reads 'Mê mou aptou', which means either 'let me go', or 'do not hold me'. Jesus must have said to Mary that she should not stop him on his way to his father. The Latin Vulgate translation chose for the *Noli me tangere* interpretation, which the KJV Bible translators in turn copied as 'touch me not.'40

Interesting speculation on the scene in the garden is shown in the following two posts.

1.   Fr. Sean Mullen;

Rembrandt painted two pictures of the scene in the garden. In the earlier version, Mary is kneeling at the top of a set of steps that lead to an open tomb. In front of her is the jar in which she carries the burial spices. Two angels are seated inside the dark cave like tomb. In this painting the artist portrays Jesus dressed like a Renaissance gardener in a white robe and bathed in warm light which is rising over the distant towers of the Jerusalem temple. In his hand is a spade and tucked into his belt is a knife or pruning shears. He is wearing a broad floppy hat which would have been worn by someone who spends long hours outside in the sun. As Rembrandt paints Jesus, he looks like a gardener and in fact his Jesus probably has dirt under his fingernails.

In his later version, Rembrandt presents the more conventional depiction--the one that conveys the clear message that Mary was mistaken.

Nevertheless, in the earlier version he does not make this assertion

We do not know if a gardener would ever have been in the vicinity of the tomb. Nevertheless, the possibility is all that matters. The conventional way of describing the encounter focuses on the error of misidentification. Nevertheless, Rembrandt presents the possibility that Jesus is both the gardener and the Risen Christ. All you have to allow for is the passage of time; and to see that Rembrandt was not interested in painting an historical representation of that first Easter morning. No, in a very real way, Rembrandt was painting an Easter morning for his own time, a contemporary Easter, with a contemporary Mary Magdalene, contemporary angels, and, of course a contemporary Jesus, who is right here with us even though he happens also to be a gardener. . . . Those who are only looking for Jesus in someone who matches their own expectations of what he should look like are bound to have rare sightings of the Lord, if any at all. But those who are on the lookout for gardeners-- or for anyone who might bear the image of Christ to them-well; they are bound to have many encounters with the living Lord, who, after all, has constituted his Body in the world by calling many people together in his church.

The great value of Rembrandt's suggestion that Jesus is both the gardener and the Risen Christ is that he invites us to think not only of all the *places* where we have failed to see Jesus, but of all the *people* in whom we have failed to see Jesus." Just as Jesus gardens Mary by calling her by her name and sending her to proclaim the Gospel, he is doing the same for us.*41*

2. The Veritas community in Lancaster, Pennsylvania broadens discussion of the passage in this way:

"John's gospel has something to communicate about humanity and the whole cosmos . . . John wants us to understand that Jesus was with God before the creation of the world and then chose to become part of God's earth as a human being. Jesus' life not only enters into cosmic history, but somehow affects all of creation itself."

The post from this community also presents us with Discussion questions as a way to deepen our exploration of this passage:

Discussion Questions:

1. *What thoughts, comments, insights, questions, etc. do you have about the passage or the message?*
2. *What is the significance of Jesus being confused as the gardener? What is the role of a gardener and how does that tie in ultimately with Jesus, and then by definition with those of us who call ourselves followers of Jesus?*
3. *What does new creation look like in our world? Share a story or two of examples of new creation/resurrection happening in*

your life, a life of a friend, or in the world at large. How can we participate in new creation?

4. So how should you and I live as individuals should and as a community of faith that seeks to live out resurrection/new creation. Give us some concrete ideas and thoughts. 42

The richness of garden narratives and artistic depictions.

Theologian Wes Howard-Brook broadens reflection on biblical gardens when he makes these observations:

Mary thinks it is the gardener that is asking the same question that the Angels in the tomb asked her, and then adding his own: 'Woman, why are you weeping? Whom are you seeking?' The narrator tells us, 'Thinking it was the gardener . . . 'This put us deeply into the ambiguity of biblical gardens, places both of intimacy and betrayal, both in Genesis and in John (18:2) Will Mary's encounter in the garden lead to intimacy or be just another betrayal? What can she possibly say to this "gardener?*43*

This statement brings to mind the experience of Suzanna in the Garden which illustrates the garden as a place of intimacy and betrayal, Daniel 13.

Suzanna is the stunning wife of a wealthy Babylonian Jew, Joachim. Her beauty attracts two elders—Judges who frequently visit their home and, beginning to desire her, plot to catch her alone in her garden, where she bathes in the afternoon. When she dismisses her maids and has them lock the gate, the men come out of hiding and demand that she lie with them. If she denies them, they will say she was with a young man. Although conflicted in her choices, Suzanna decides to refuse them. In return they lie about the situation, and because they are believed, she is condemned to death. She turns to prayer, however, and God intervenes, sending Daniel, a young man who cries out, "I will have no part in the death of this woman" (13:46). Daniel rebukes the people for condemning Suzanna and cleverly traps the Elders in their lies. Suzanna is saved and the elders are condemned to death.

The Garden in Art and Scripture.

In my research I came upon this interesting post by Fr. Peter Schineller, SJ. What follows is a summary of his blog presentation which he generously gave permission to publish.**44**

He begins his blog, *Jesus the Gardener*, noting that "Jesus is the Good Shepherd, the King of Kings, our Lord and Savior. He is the Messiah, the Way, the Truth and the Life. These are among the many important names and titles we give to Jesus Christ. There is one more worth reflecting upon especially as Christians move to Holy Week and Easter, the most solemn of the Church Year, namely Jesus the Gardener."

Jesus the Gardener: "The artist Albrecht Durer captures that scene in his etching entitled 'Christ as Gardener'. Jesus wears the cap of a gardener at work, and carries a shovel, about to go to work. Is it not fitting that Jesus risen in glory appears to Mary as the gardener in the Garden of the Resurrection?"

Garden in the Scriptures: Schineller has a lengthy list of the various citations of "Garden" in Genesis.

Garden of Suffering: "After the Last Supper, the Paschal Meal on Holy Thursday with his disciples, Jesus proceeds to the Garden of Gethsemane . . . There was a garden there, and he and his disciples entered it" (Jn. 18:1). John adds that it was familiar, "because Jesus had often met there with his disciples" (Jn. 18: 2). He prays there in great agony. He courageously commits himself to do the Father's will, even to death. Later, in that garden, the soldiers capture Jesus and his imprisonment and trial follows . . . On Good Friday there is another garden . . . The place of death is a garden place. There Jesus dies into his Father's hands.

Garden of the Resurrection: "Jesus very fittingly and beautifully appears to Mary Magdalene as the Gardener. The garden is the place where the glory of God is revealed. Gardens are places of new and recurrent life, where plants, flowers, shrubs, vegetables come to life, springtime after springtime. The gardener is the one who oversees and does his part so the cycle of life reoccurs. The gardener plants and prunes, digs, fertilizes and waters so that trees and plants bear fruit, fruit in abundance."

Heaven the Garden of God: "The Book of Revelation describes heaven as the new Jerusalem, the heavenly city with mighty walls and ornate gates. The lamp or light in it is Jesus Christ the Lamb (Rev. 21). It also speaks of heaven as a garden, with the "river of life-giving water . . . which flowed down the middle of the streets. On either side of the river grew the trees of life." (Rev. 22:1-2)

Some Miscellaneous Reflections on Gardens.

In his book *Between Two Gardens* the biblical scholar James B Nelson states:

So, we Christians today live between the times. Or perhaps we live between the gardens. One garden is the Erotic Garden that depicted in the Song of Songs. This much-misinterpreted piece of scripture is a biblical love poem celebrating the joys of erotic love between a woman and a man.

The Garden of Eden depicted in the Yahwist creation story, Genesis 2-3, is different. Here the results of the fall into sexual dualism are evident. The whole material world participates in the fall. Work itself is cursed and childbirth marked with alienating pain. The writer of this garden story seems to depict the woman as derivative of the man.

In all this, there is something of a literary irony. The Garden of Eden, which is mythic, seems to give the more realistic portrayal of the human sexual story, whereas the real historical tale of two lovers, the Canticles, seems to border on sexual myth . . . one might ask, which is "realistic" our alienation or our possibility? *45*

Some Final Thoughts on Gardens from a Journalist.

Gardeners, like their subjects, ripen over time and experience eventually drive out the silliest notions about how to approach the soil. It may be true, as Painter Dash believes that for the moment gardening has become a gorgeous new American toy, the latest vehicle for social climbing. If so, that in time is sure to change. "It is possible we will garden on American terms," he predicts. "We will make brave and beautiful gardens with hardier plants. And because we are a generous country, our gardens will be very generous and robust with a snap of the wilderness about them . . . perhaps aiming at what we lost.

In the meantime, we will revel in paradoxes, in gardens that cost nothing and those that cost a king's ransom, in the gardens that consume all our waking hours alone in the gardens of the cities surrounded by thickets of steel, in the gardens grown out of folly and philosophy. We will approach with awe the ceremonies of the out-of-doors and become in the process less brittle, more wise, managing miracles. We may even become as Thomas Jefferson once modestly christened all his fellow gardeners, the chosen people of God.*46*

Chapter Four

"Fanciful Speculation" or "Fruitful Contemplation?"

THIS CHAPTER IS THE LAST of Section one. It contains a variety of posts which have enriched me. As I read them, I found myself enjoying both speculation and contemplation. Sometimes the lines between the two seemed to blur, but I enjoyed this journey. My hope is that you the reader will be enriched and enjoy your journey. This chapter is also a transition to Section two, titled Jesus Gardens me. Actual Journeys and Pilgrimages are a large part of the next chapter. This chapter too is a journey and pilgrimage and includes some of my own musings.

(As I was in the last stages of getting my manuscript prepared for publication, I came upon this book Mary Magdalen (Myth and Metaphor) by Susan Haskins. It is 518 pages of research with almost 90 pages of footnotes. On the back cover is this quote from the Evening Standard: "The lasting image of the book is profound and moving that of a real woman in a garden talking to Christ by a tomb, unchanged in spite of centuries of distortion." The subtitle of the book (Myth and Metaphor) seems to me to complement the title I have given this chapter.47

+++

Dr. Jo-Ann A. Brant mentions in her commentary on John's Gospel: "That Jesus has left his burial clothes in the tomb might provoke fanciful speculation that Jesus has borrowed the gardener's clothes. Rembrandt depicts this possibility in his painting *The Resurrected Lord Appears to Mary Magdalene.*"**48**

++

In 1990 art historian, Georges Didi-Huberman published a monograph on Fra Angelico, spending considerable time on his *Noli me tangere*, especially its red flowers, which he reads as a figural displacement of Christ's stigmata (nail wounds).**49**

++

'Don't touch me', says Jesus to Mary Magdalene, recoiling. Mary has come to the grave that morning to embalm the body of Christ. To her amazement, Jesus is walking around alive. She first mistakes him for the gardener, which is why Titian has him holding a spade.

Irony has it that the crux of the story is presumably based on a translation error. The Greek source text reads *'Mê mou aptou'*, which mean either 'let me go', or 'do not hold me.' Jesus must have said to Mary that she should not stop him on his way to his father. The Latin Vulgate translation chose for the *Noli me tangere* interpretation, which the KJV Bible translators in turn copied as 'touch me not.'**50**

++

On the blog, Art & Theology *Revitalizing the Christian imagination through painting, poetry, music, and more,* several comments were posted.

"I think one of *the beautiful things about iconography is how there is the ability to depict things not necessarily as they appear, but as they actually are.* One might say that Mary Magdalene indeed saw Christ as He truly is (even though she did not recognize Him), as the true Gardener."

"I like Francesco de Mura's version of "*Noli Me Tangere*" –Jesus is carrying a hoe and looks startlingly corporeal for one who is on the way to ascending; as in many representations of this scene, there's an interesting tension between earth and heaven, between the earthly and the spiritual."

The diversity, imagination, and creativity in the above three posts fascinate me. "Figural displacement", "based on a translation error", "*beautiful things about iconography*" and finally "tension between earth and heaven, between the earthly and the spiritual." Perhaps they illustrate the presence of the Holy Spirit, who blows where she/he wills, to use a Scriptural phrase.*51*

+++

On the feast of St. Mary Magdalene in 2018, Fr. Sean Mullen preached on the Gospel passage, John 20 the Appearance to Magdalene. Pointing out that Rembrandt had painted two different depictions of this scene, he refers to the scene as a "preserved ancient moment", and went on to say:

> If there was always the possibility of a gardener hanging around the empty tomb, one way of finding contemporary significance in this ancient resurrection scene is to conclude that there is always the chance of getting it wrong and mistaking Jesus for the gardener-- this is the conventional way of conveying the encounter artistically-- to focus on the error of mis-identification.
>
> But there is another way of finding present meaning in this preserved ancient moment. And that way of seeing things is to suppose that wherever there is the possibility of a gardener, so to speak, there is also the possibility of

encountering the risen Jesus. And Rembrandt seems to have imagined this possibility, the possibility that Mary is not entirely wrong about the gardener: that Jesus is both the gardener, and the risen Christ, too.

In order to imagine such a thing, you do not have to suggest that Jesus is some kind of body snatcher, who might invade the body of an unsuspecting gardener, like some messianic parasite inhabiting its host's body. All you have to allow for is the passage of time; and to see that Rembrandt was not interested in painting an historical representation of that first Easter morning. No, in a very real way, Rembrandt was painting an Easter morning for his own time, a contemporary Easter, with a contemporary Mary Magdalene, contemporary angels, and, of course a contemporary Jesus, who is right here with us even though he happens also to be a gardener."

Fr. Sean then offers practical gems to apply the passage to our lived experience. Here is a taste: Rembrandt "invites us to think not only of all the *places* where we have failed to see Jesus, but of all the *people* in whom we have failed to see Jesus." There is much more to ponder in this sermon, but he concludes:

Since we hardly know what to look for any more, when we are looking for Jesus . . . and since many have given up looking altogether . . . but since we are all of us headed somehow toward the darkness of the grave. . . I find it a matter of hope that there is every possibility that Jesus is right behind me, that he has been here all along, since there has always been the possibility of a gardener, that he is wearing a broad hat, so exaggerated that there is room for me and for you beneath its wide brim, that he knows us each by name, and that, yes, he is the gardener, too. And with him comes the light. *52*

++++++++++++++++++++++++++++++++++++++

Award winning, Andrew Hudgins—inspired by the imagination of visual artists—wrote a poem called "Christ as a Gardener"**53**

The boxwoods planted in the park spell LIVE.
I never noticed it until they died.
Before, the entwined green had smudged the word
unreadable. And when they take their own advice
again — come spring, come Easter — no one will know
a word is buried in the leaves. I love the way
that Mary thought her resurrected Lord
a gardener. It wasn't just the broad-brimmed hat
and muddy robe that fooled her: he was that changed.
He looks across the unturned field, the riot
Of unscythed grass, the smattering of wildflowers.
Before he can stop himself, he's on his knees.
He roots up stubborn weeds, pinches the suckers,
deciding order here — what lives, what dies,
and how. But it goes deeper even than that.
His hands burn and his bare feet smolder. He longs
To lie down inside the long, dew-moist furrows
and press his pierced side and his broken forehead
into the dirt. But he's already done it —
passed through one death and out the other side.
He laughs. He kicks his bright spade in the earth
and turns it over. Spring flashes by, then harvest.
Beneath his feet, seeds dance into the air.
They rise, and he, not noticing, ascends
on midair steppingstones of dandelion,
of milkweed, thistle, cattail, and goldenrod.

++++++++++++++++++++++++++++++++++++++

In my present research into the scene of Mary Magdalene in the garden, I found myself humming Oh Susanna. I have no idea why this was happening, but I was drawn to look up the lyrics. Here is what I discovered.

"Oh! Susanna" is not only one of Stephen Foster's best-known songs, but also one of the best-known American tunes. No American song had ever sold more than 5,000 copies before. "Oh! Susanna" sold over 100,000.

Here are the lyrics:

I come from Alabama with my banjo on my knee,
I'm going to Louisiana, my true love for to see.
It rained all night the day I left, the weather it was dry
The sun so hot I froze to death, Susanna, don't you cry.
Chorus
Oh! Susanna, oh don't you cry for me. For I come from Alabama
with my banjo on my knee.

John's Gospel is a bit like the song. Now before you think I have gone off the deep end, let me briefly explain. In chapter 20 alone, there are twists, turns, and paradoxes to rival some of the contradictory lyrics of "Oh Susanna". This morning I explored the Garden passage in my favorite commentary on John's Gospel, *Becoming Children of God* by Wes Howard-Brook. "When Jesus calls Mary by her name, Mary calls Jesus by the intimate, yet lesser title, Rabbouni. (Twice prior to this exchange, she has spoken of Jesus as Lord). There is a *total difference in the relationship.*"

Howard-Brook strongly notes some of the twists and turns and paradox. "From *soudarian* (facecloth) to angels in white, to Jesus himself, the fact of resurrection emerges like a photographic print in the darkness. Suddenly without the slightest notice, the narrative affirms the greatest theological reality in all human experience, as if it was as expectable an event as the movement from night to day."**54**

++

John Donaghy, a lay missioner with the Catholic Diocese of Santa Rosa de Copán, Honduras, writes a blog, *Walk the Way* which offers reflections related to historic events, witnesses to peace and justice, and the daily lectionary readings. On March 31, 2013, Donaghy posted this picture by Fra Angelico and commented:

After having told Peter and John that the tomb was empty, Mary of Magdala returned to the tomb. Two angels there asked her why she is weeping. "Because they have taken away my Lord . . . Dismayed, she turns asks a man she encounters, "Where have you put him?" It is Jesus but she does not recognize him until he calls her by name. She thinks he is the gardener. In Fra Angelico's fresco, Jesus *is* a gardener, carrying a hoe over his shoulder. Could Jesus really be a gardener? Could he be the risen one who seeks to restore the garden of our souls, as he gives new life and hope to Mary of Magdala? Could he be the risen one who seeks to restore the garden of our world, torn by death and violence, so that we might live more like our first parents in the Garden of Eden? Let us open our hearts to the gardener who prunes, fertilizes, and waters us by his death and resurrection. Let us commit ourselves to live as gardeners of this world, seeking to bring integrity, peace, and compassion to our broken world. Perhaps that is how we can celebrate the risen Lord, the gardener.

In another post on April 22, 2014, Donaghy reflects on John 20:11-18 and includes the painting of Fra Angelico as he did the prior year, that of the Dominican friar's cells in San Marco Convent in Florence.

In today's Gospel (John 20: 11-18), Mary Magdalen mistakes Jesus for a gardener. However, is it really a mistake? Is not Jesus the gardener of souls? Nevertheless, even more, is not the Garden the place where humans first encountered God? In Genesis 3, we read that God walked with Adam and Eve in the Garden of Eden. Nevertheless, they hid after abusing the garden, eating from the tree of knowledge of good and evil. At the serpent's suggestion, they ate the fruit because they wanted to be like gods. In the Garden of the Tomb, Mary Magdalene encounters the Lord Jesus who calls her by name.

The garden that was lost is now encountered. The relation between God and humans is now restored. The hope is that the relation between God and all creation is now also restored. God has initiated this but, like Mary Magdalen, we are called, to pass on the message of the risen Lord, of the promise of resurrection for God's people and of the renewed creation. What a fitting message for Earth Day. Let us work with the Gardener to restore some signs of the Garden of Eden on God's good earth. *55*

+++

"She mistook him for the gardener"

Posted on <u>April 5, 2016</u> by <u>Victoria Emily Jones</u>

Artists—mainly from the fifteenth and sixteenth centuries—have latched onto this detail of mistaken identity, representing Jesus carrying gardening tools, like a shovel or a hoe, and sometimes sporting a floppy gardener's hat. A few artists, such as Lavinia Fontana, Rembrandt, and the illuminators of the book of hours and passional, have even showed Jesus in full-out gardener's getup. In her *Commentary on John*, Dr. Jo-Ann A. Brant mentions that the fact that Jesus left his burial clothes in the tomb, coupled with Mary's confusion, might provoke the "fanciful speculation" that Jesus actually borrowed the gardener's clothes. Nevertheless, a different understanding is more likely behind the artistic representations; read on.

The portrayal of Jesus as a gardener is not meant to suggest that Jesus was literally gardening that day—though he might have been, and that is amusing to think of. Rather, it alludes to his role as one who "plants" us and grows us. He gets his hands dirty in the soil of our hearts, bringing us to life and cultivating us with care so that we flourish. Artists— mainly from the fifteenth and sixteenth centuries—have latched onto this detail of mistaken identity, representing Jesus carrying gardening tools, like a shovel or a hoe, and sometimes sporting a floppy gardener's hat.

According to Franco Mormando, whose research involves the religious sources of Renaissance and Baroque Catholic art, Jesus the gardener was a traditional theme of orthodox scriptural exegesis and popular preaching whose origins can be traced back to patristic times. In a 2009 article for America magazine, he writes:

Mary's misidentification was meant to remind us, so the pre-modern exegetes taught, of a spiritual reality: Jesus is the gardener of the human soul, eradicating evil, noxious vegetation and planting, as St. Gregory the Great says, "The flourishing seeds of virtue." Although today out of circulation, this teaching was disseminated [in the fourteenth through eighteenth centuries] in such popular, authoritative texts as Ludolph of Saxony's *Life of Christ* (a book that played a crucial role in St. Ignatius Loyola's conversion) and [starting in the seventeenth century] Jesuit Cornelius a Lapide's *Great Commentary on Scripture*.

The Bible makes explicit the connection between God the Father and gardening. Genesis 2:8 tells us he was the world's first gardener: "And the Lord God planted a garden in Eden, in the east, and there he put the man whom he had formed". The prophets sometimes wrote of God's gardening in a metaphoric sense—for example, in Isaiah 61:11: "For as the earth brings forth its sprouts, / and as a garden causes what is sown in it to sprout up, / so the Lord God will cause righteousness and praise / to sprout up before all the nations." Or, Jeremiah 24:6, in which God says of the exiles from Judah, "I will build them up, and not tear them down; I will plant them, and not pluck them up." Furthermore, Jesus' parable from John 15 casts God as a vinedresser.

John's Gospel, though, goes even further to ascribe this role to Jesus, and to present his resurrection as the genesis of something new. For example, the prologue to his Gospel starts, "In the beginning . . . ," an obvious echo of the prologue to Genesis. In 19:41, he mentions that Jesus was buried in a garden, and in chapter 20, that he was found walking around in it. He mentions twice that Jesus rose on "the first day" of the week, as if this were the first day of a new creation (cf. Genesis 1:3–5). Then he has Mary mistake Jesus for the gardener. When taken in concert with Paul's conception of Jesus as the Second Adam (Romans 5:12–21; 1 Corinthians 15:21–22, 45), these allusions suggest that Jesus is the gardener of the new Eden, doing what Adam could not do. His resurrection broke ground in this garden, marking the beginning of a massive restoration project.

That is why Jesus is so often found toting a shovel in the resurrection art of Renaissance and Baroque Europe. He is the caretaker of humanity, bending down to bring us up, to make us full, healthy, and beautiful. Charles Spurgeon preached a sermon on the topic back in 1882, in which he declares: "Behold, the church is Christ's Eden, watered by the river of life, and so fertilized that all manner of fruits are brought forth unto God; and he, our second Adam, walks in this spiritual Eden to dress it and to keep it; and so by a type we see that we are right in "supposing him to be the gardener."

A few artists have even shown Jesus in full-out gardener's getup.

Lavinia Fontana (Italian, 1552–1614), Noli me tangere, 1581. Oil on canvas, 80 × 65.6 cm. Uffizi Gallery, Florence, Italy.

I'm curious to know whether any modern artists have exegeted John's text in the same way—that is, portraying Jesus as a gardener in his appearance to Mary Magdalene. (*Victoria Emily Jones*)

Back in 2010 Jyoti Sahi, not a highly recognized contemporary artist, posted an oil painting on his blog along with three others under the heading "The Resurrection." In it Jesus carries an oversize scythe while Mary anoints his feet, just as she had done a week earlier, when she had shed tears in anticipation of his death (John 12:1–8). The outline around her is reminiscent of a kernel of wheat. Jyoti Sahi (Indian, 1944–), *The Resurrection*. Oil on canvas

Most people associate scythe-wielding figures in art with the Grim Reaper—that is, Death—due to an iconography that stretches all the way back to the fourteenth century. But the Bible associates scythes

with Jesus, the lord of the harvest (Matthew 3:12, ;Matthew 13:24, Revelation), the harvest being the end of the world. Only those who have rejected Jesus need fear his Second Coming, for those who have grown in his word will be gathered up into heaven. This painting in particular reminds me of *Psalm 126:5*: "They that sow in tears shall reap in joy. Mary had wept penitently over her sin, and then later over the impending execution of her Lord, and still again, at his grave, but now, because of his Resurrection, she enters into his presence with shouts of joy, and even more cause for worship.**56**

++

The first parable of Mark in his Gospel also speaks of the "sickle". Mark 4: 26-29 "26 He also said, "The kingdom of God is as if someone would scatter seed on the ground, 27 and would sleep and rise night and day, and the seed would sprout and grow, he does not know how. 28 The earth produces of itself, first the stalk, then the head, then the full grain in the head. 29 But when the grain is ripe, at once he goes in with his sickle, because the harvest has come.""

++

Article in Sisters Today, Meeting the Gardener.

Teresa M. Donohue, CSJP wrote an article in the periodical Sisters Today, "A Congregational Experience Program: Meeting the Gardener;" in which she describes the Congregational Experience Program. She offers her personal reflections:

The first morning of the program, the reading at prayer was John: 20:11-18, where Mary meets the gardener. As we named our hopes and fears, my hope as well as my fear was of meeting the gardener. My prayer and my relationship with God grew and deepened throughout the program; I truly did meet the gardener and was graced to recognize the gardener. I reflected on having met the gardener at my center and to what that was calling me. It was this very gardener who was calling me to the ministry of social justice, who worked with us, and whose Spirit was the source of our wisdom and hope.

My life has changed: I have changed, and I feel I will continue to change as much as I allow the Spirit to live within me and listen to the gardener. Having met the gardener, I am called to be radically open: open to growth, to new concepts and ideas; open to face uncertainty and fear, open to face my value addictions; open to the possibility of being misunderstood, even rejected.

And so I hope to continue to meet and recognize the gardener and to listen to what the gardener is saying, knowing that such a meeting involved change, risk, vulnerability, conversion and transformation—yet brings new life, new hope, and new promise."

Teresa's experience reflects for me Mary Magdalene's experience with the gardener, and my own.**57**

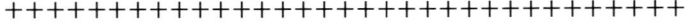

In a blog on the web site Episcopal Café, Dr. Dana Kramer-Rolls posted Jesus the Gardener.

Why the gardener? Just a case of mistaken identity? Not likely, especially from the Gospel of John, a gospel of complex mature Trinitarian theology, expressed in powerful language, and often in opaque statements. The importance of Jesus the Gardener is often left behind as the narrative of

Jesus' first appearances unfolds. But the gardener is important, neither trivial nor accidental.

He knows her name, this Gardener, as he knows the
names of each and every one of us. Mary stayed. Mary loved.
Mary stayed and wept.

Jesus could not even allow Mary to touch him. This is
a turning point of the Resurrection narrative in John. Jesus
not yet ascended, not touchable.

Mysteries are mysteries for a reason, and the reason
is not reason, as we know it from science and philosophy.
They are there to touch our deepest heart. As they touched
Mary's when she heard her name but was forbidden to touch
the one she loved more than anything or anyone else. She
obeyed, but she must have been hurting, confused, through
the relief and love she felt from just seeing him. As we may
see glimpses of him, love him, but cannot touch him in this
life.

Did she ever see the Resurrected Christ again in this
life? We do not know. Did she receive the Spirit, as did the
men? We do not know, but I cannot see how she could not
have. Did she learn in the Spirit how to spend her life in the
presence of her Lord, the Holy One, in prayer, devotion,
spreading his word, as she knew it? We do not know.

What about us on Easter, after a long and moving Vigil,
perhaps baptisms welcoming new souls into the Body of
Christ? Perhaps on Sunday with a large rowdy family, joyous,
if somewhat secular, waiting for the feast, which follows the
Feast of God? What did we see? Paul says in one Corinthians
15:14, "and if Christ has not been raised, then our proclamation has been in vain and your faith has been in vain". Can we
put ourselves by the tomb with Mary and see the Gardener,

and hear him call us by name? Can we answer, "Teacher"? "My Lord and my God"? He is risen. He is risen indeed. **58**

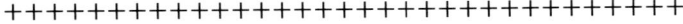

Dudley Hall, president of Successful Christian Living Ministries, is committed to communicating the essentials of the Christian faith in an easy to grasp fashion, evidenced by his posts on the Stream podcasts.

"Jesus has many titles. But seldom do we call him the gardener. Mary Magdalene mistook Jesus for a gardener when she went to the tomb on Sunday morning and couldn't find Jesus' body. She asked him where the body had been taken so that she could attend to it. He revealed himself as the resurrected Lord. But there is a real sense in which her mistaken assumption was correct: that he was the gardener."

As the sermon continues, Dudley Hall takes a brief look at Salvation History. He refers to Adam as the first Gardener in the Garden of Eden. "God had a plan, but we know that Adam and Eve frustrated God's plan and they were exiled from the Garden. There were other consequences as well. A curse came upon all the earth because of their sin, and the garden of the earth felt the effects of neglect, including all societal structures."

Later, Hall notes, God chose the descendants of Abraham as his partners and gave them a land to manage. They too sinned and were exiled into Babylonian captivity.

Then, God sent his Son. He appeared as the final Adam, and as corporate Israel, to accomplish what neither of them could. After he had paid the cost of their failure, he arose from the dead — in a garden, as the first fruits of a new creation. Those who are "in Him" are assigned to manage the new garden. After his ascension, the disciples were sent to the whole world to herald the presence of the Kingdom of God. This is the mission of the church in our day. It is what we do in the meantime based on what Jesus has already done while we wait until we receive resurrected bodies in the culmination of the new creation. We are working in his garden under his loving rule. We are privileged to be his partners sharing in his life and mission. We live with confidence in him though we face daunting tasks while living in a world that reels from the chaos of sin. The great news is that He is already on the throne and no one rivals him. He wins, and we share in his victory. As we glimpse at the garden through the eyes of John, the human author of The Revelation (chapters 21-22), we see the garden in the final form.

Let's identify our personal gardens and get to work."**59**

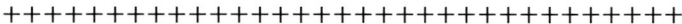

So--again, we can ask our exploratory questions after our journey through "Fanciful Speculation" or "Fruitful Contemplation?"

Could Jesus really be a gardener?

Could he be the risen one who seeks to restore the garden of our souls, as he gives new life and hope to Mary of Magdala?

Could he be the risen one who seeks to restore the garden of our world, torn by death and violence, so that we might live more like our first parents in the Garden of Eden?

Let us open our hearts to the gardener who prunes, fertilizes, and waters us by his death and resurrection.

Let us commit ourselves to live as gardeners of this world, seeking to bring integrity, peace, and compassion to our broken world.

Perhaps that is how we can celebrate the risen Lord, the gardener.

SECTION TWO:

Jesus Gardens me.

Chapter Five

Autobiographical Scan.

Father Richard Rohr, OFM, wrote two weeks of reflections on Jesus of Nazareth. He began them asserting: "Simply put, God reveals God's self to us through what unfolds as our life, along with every visible thing around us."*60*

Fr. Michael Casey states: "It is by reflecting on our own personal history that we begin to see God's action in our lives—creating us, preserving us from many misfortunes, and endowing us with so many benefits. Slowly we begin to glimpse this overwhelming benevolence in our regard".*61*

Professor Luke Timothy Johnson offers his perspective on what our experience with God brings: "Science and technology are unable to express fear and loathing, desire and love, alienation and reconciliation. They cannot comprehend, much less create, the art, music, poetry, and drama that liberate and elevate human lives. How much more is myth necessary for the expression of the experience of God's presence and power in creation?"**62**

The Easter Moment of Jesus and Mary Magdalene in the garden tomb area-- is it myth? Does it describe a real event? Does it matter?

What is your reaction to these questions?
After reading the two aspects of God's actions in our life: 1) The benevolence of God and 2) what science and technology bring, if you

were to start making a list of God's actions in your life, would you start with the first or the second? Which list would be longer? Why?

I like the image of Jesus the itinerant preacher cultivating Mary Magdalene as a gardener. It was an inspiration calling me to tell my story, Jesus Gardens Me.

For a week, I was on retreat at Willka Tika Guest House—a garden paradise in the Sacred Valley of Peru, where Seven Chakra healing gardens dominate the grounds. A Spiral (a variation of the Labyrinth) is one of the healing gardens which gave me an experience I'd never had previously while walking various Labyrinths. Midway through walking the Spiral, I came upon a quite large rock blocking the way straight ahead. The path curved to go around the rock. At the center of the Spiral, the path turned to go back in the opposite direction. On this return when I came upon the rock, there was no obstacle and I could walk directly ahead with no detour. Jesus seemed to be guiding, inspiring me to put in writing some details of how I have felt Jesus gardening me in my life.

How this gardener would inspire me-- I had no idea. Nevertheless, I began by making two lists. People whom I have taken advantage were on the first list. The second was of those people who have (advantaged me) positively influenced me. (As I write this now, I am reminded how similar this step for me is to the fourth step of Alcoholics Anonymous: "Made a searching and fearless moral inventory of ourselves").

I began with the first list (people of whom I have taken advantage.) and rejoiced in discerning only five names. I started the second list and to my wondering surprise, that one kept getting longer and longer.

The first name that came to mind surprised me: Hutch, who had been my baseball coach in Pony League. However, Hutch was more than a baseball coach. From 1952-1956 I attended Divine Heart Seminary High School. Summers I would be home playing baseball, my passion. During the summer of my junior year, I was selected for the Pony league all-stars. I was an infielder who seldom let a ball get by me. Because I was younger and shorter than many of the players on the all-star team,

I was moved from shortstop to second base. It was very exciting. At the start of the senior year, it was the custom to return to the seminary early to help prepare the building for the coming school year. After one of my last games Hutch, carrying a new baseball, came up to me, a serious look on his face. He said, "I think you are making the right choice to continue on the path to being a priest, but I just want you to have this baseball and if you ever change your mind, bring the baseball back to me and I will help you to a baseball career."

Have you had an experience that gave you a certain direction on your journey of life? Have you ever made an inventory of your life?

Who would be the first person on your list of people who have positively impacted you?

After finishing college, our provincial asked several of us to take time out from our preparation and studies for priesthood and teach in two high school seminaries--two of us to the new high school seminary opening in Lenox, Massachusetts.

During the summers we began studies for Master's degrees in various subjects, and I was to major in Latin and Greek, for which I was ill prepared. I made it through the course work and Comprehensive exam, but never finished the dissertation—no M.A.

However, summer school at Catholic University in Washington, D.C. had many pluses, one of which was that the Religious Education department under Fr. Gerry Sloyan brought in outstanding speakers in theology, liturgy, and psychology. One of the faculty members was the gracious and warm, Fr. Eugene Kennedy, a Maryknoll psychologist for whom I served every morning in the crypt of the National Shrine of the Immaculate Conception. One day I asked to speak with him and he invited me to his office, where I told him that I was concerned because as Latin and World History teacher, assistant prefect, and athletic director, I liked some of the students better than I liked others. When he asked, "So how many students do you like?" I answered about 25. He said,

"Well then don't worry about it". As I look back it seems such simple and wise advice. My concern vanished.

Can you recall an experience in your life when you either were asked to do something or chose to do something that did not directly influence your life journey, but a tangential aspect proved to be very important?

Can you point to someone who took a youthful concern of yours and helped you through it with wise words?

Another person who gave me a positive direction was the personnel director of the U.S. province of the Priests of the Sacred Heart. He visited me when I was pastor in St. Rose of Lima parish in inner city Detroit, where everything in our neighborhood was broken: housing that had missing or broken windows, houses stripped of all copper wiring, everywhere broken glass, broken people, drug addicts, and people with severe mental issues. Two German police dogs prowled at night in our rectory, church, and school building. A Felician sister friend told me one day, "You are getting very hardened". When John visited with me, he knew I was depressed. I told him if I were an alcoholic I would know where to get help, but I did not know how to get help for my state of mind. He said he knew a bit about a program called The House of Affirmation. Thus, began a healing process. Following a three-day evaluation at a center in Massachusetts, I was invited to spend time at the House of Affirmation in Montara, California. This experience got me in touch with some of my self-defeating behaviors. It helped me with my depression. What a blessing that proved to be.

Can you point to individuals in your life who helped you face a certain crisis?

The sixth person on my list was Jerome Clifford. After my stay at the California program, he encouraged me to study for a Master's degree in scripture at Catholic Theological Union in Chicago. Unfortunately, my scripture studies at Sacred Heart School of Theology had been woefully inadequate, the professor claimed to be keeping up with developments in his field, but his classes did not demonstrate that. At Catholic Theological Union I was blessed with several professors who positively impacted me: Don Senior, Carrol Stuhlmueller, Eugene LaVerdiere, Sister Carolyn Osiek and a rabbi whose name I can't recall. Their classes were stimulating, challenging, and inspiring.

Several Religious Sisters, for their friendship and sharing are also on my list of those having a positive impact on me. My mom and dad come to mind as well and of course my brother and two sisters.

Another on my list was Fr. Patrick Cremer, a gentle giant, who taught us dogmatic theology. Though our scripture courses were a disaster, he was translating *Christ the Sacrament of the Encounter with God* for one of our dogmatic courses. It was fantastic.

I am not sure if, subsequently, it was Fr. Cremer or someone else, who led me to read the book *Apologetics and the Biblical Christ* by Avery Dulles, SJ. My previous Apologetics course had been taught by the same Scripture professor whose courses I detested and who used a manual that argued from proof texts. Dulles in contrast offered scriptural material, which destroyed the manual's approach and offered an exciting vision of the subject. (The influence of these two texts made me more aware of how powerful books are in shaping our learning.)

Pondering the aforementioned significant people and their positive and powerful impact on my life I am reminded that we are sometimes encouraged to count our blessings. This exercise has been just that, a remembered counting of some of the many and special blessings I have received in my life. And, of course I am very much aware that there have been many others who could be included in this list.

Have you experienced insight and excitement through a book or books that inspirited you?

Questions for Reflection

1. Am I able to make a list of individual people who have had a negative effect on my life?
2. Am I able to make a list of significant people who have had a positive impact on my life?
3. What kinds of feelings did this process bring up for me?
4. Have some behaviors, weaknesses, or failures emerged which I need to work on?

Chapter Six

Consciousness Raising Trips.

A QUESTION I HAVE OFTEN pondered is "What have been other influences in my life journey of Jesus' gardening me?"

My personal response to the question led me to recall that various travel experiences have strongly affected me.

At the beginning of Chapter 5 I quoted Fr. Rohr saying to me and to you "Simply put, God reveals God's self to us through what unfolds as our life, along with every visible thing around us."**63**

As I was ruminating, I remembered that, though I am not a person who regularly journals, I have rather extensive notes in several different journals for these trips. I had not looked at them for several years, though the memories clearly made a deep impression on me. I would like to share them here along with the influence they have had on my life. I also accompany them with reflection questions.

1. Study Trip To The Holy Land, Turkery And Greece. 1976

Let me begin with the origin of this trip. While perusing an article in *National Geographic* magazine, I came upon a picture of the traditional Mount Sinai. "Something is calling me to go there" was a strong reaction that immediately welled up.

Thus, I was inspired to request permission from the provincial. However, I received the response that only those who will teach scripture make such trips. I was disappointed, but not deterred.

Subsequently, after finishing five years as pastor of Holy Spirit Parish in Hernando, Mississippi, some parishioners approached me asking what I would like as a departure gift. "Aha" moment: "I would like to make a study trip to the Holy Land." They were all for it. Therefore, this time I wrote the provincial, that as a going-away gift the people of the parish would like to present me with a journey to the Holy Land. It was an offer he could not refuse.

Since I wanted to visit the site I had seen in the magazine, I began to research what kinds of options were available that included visiting Mt. Sinai and I discovered one sponsored by St. Louis University and Saint Mary's University in San Antonio. It required taking the course for credit and doing some preparatory study prior to leaving. Fortunately, even with the limited resources available in Hernando, I was able to produce responses to a set of questions and thus was accepted for the tour, conducted by Fr. Charlie Miller, that included days in Israel, Turkey, and Greece. He provided each participant with a guidebook, which, together with the studies beforehand, provided a wealth of information. So, I travelled and studied for six weeks. We spent four and a half in Israel, a day and a half in Turkey and a week in Greece.

Questions for reflection

Can you look back on your life and discover a time when a dream led you to take a particular course of exploration?

Have you met with an obstacle or obstacles that got in the way of your dream?

Is there some experience that you persevered in pursuing and finally accomplished?

Is there some dream that you have discarded? What should you do about it now?

Israel

Something was pulling me to Sinai, a pull I could not resist. Fortunately, my pre-trip research had equipped me to understand better the scriptural scene. In addition, Fr. Miller, our tour leader, prepared a detailed book containing abundant information about every site we would visit. I wrote my observations (almost daily) on the blank sides of the pages.

Nevertheless, in no way was I prepared for several encounters I had. Culture shock was abundant for me on this tour.

Israel was a security state. Every bank had soldier guards with machine guns, a reality which initially was quite disorienting for me. However, as I reflected, what scared me more was how quickly I became accustomed to this reality, as our bus encountered many security stops with armed guards.

On our visit to the Allenby Bridge, connecting Israel and Jordan, as we approached, we encountered an area where Jordanian crossers were being interrogated behind barbed wire fences. However, most shocking was the way the Israeli soldiers treated the Arabs crossing for work. I witnessed them having their belongings (carried in blankets) sprawled nastily over tables for inspection. Closer to the bridge we encountered a fortified bunker with machine guns. Our guide said, "You can walk on the bridge and take pictures". As I did so, a Jordanian soldier walked toward me from the opposite side, proclaiming "no pictures, no pictures". I hastily took one anyway and quickly backtracked to the Israel side, having decided I did not want to be part of an international incident.

In our four- and one-half weeks in Israel we were cautioned where not to go. My consciousness of the struggle between Israelis and Palestinians and the difficult complexities it presents has stayed with me to this day. We traveled on Israeli buses and passed through checkpoints rapidly without any searches. The experience of those on Arab busses was completely different.

Clearly, the "two state solution" was very much alive even then. Israeli settlements, wall building, moving the capital from Tel Aviv to Jerusalem, are present realities. Bombing and retaliatory strikes are frequent. Leadership of the Palestinians is very mixed. Some leaders advocate for a peaceful solution, others advocate military aggression. I see these current realities through the experience of this trip.

Among my unforgettable experiences, one stands out. On an unplanned day a seminarian and I decided to try to walk from Anathoth (place of Jeremiah's birth) toward the isolated monastery, which we had seen on the road from Jericho to Jerusalem. He could read enough Hebrew to get us on the right bus to get from Jerusalem to Anathoth, three miles north. It was not a very large city, and it was quite easy locating a spring leading out into the wilderness where we wanted to go. We set out following it, and soon observed a group of young people from the United States who were walking toward Anathoth accompanied by armed Jewish soldiers. Moving on, we noticed that the stream of water was diminishing. We walked for more than an hour and arrived at the literal end of the water. Not surprisingly, a bit of anxiety set in. I recalled that it was in this general area that Bishop Pike evidently ran out of water, became disoriented, and died. We had to make a decision: go forward or go back. Deciding to go ahead, we did not make contact with any other people for another hour or so. Anxiety increased. Then with great relief, we heard some voices ahead of us. We came around a bend and there in front of us was a group of Jewish students from the United States and their bus. They gave us water and invited us to join them on the trip back to Jerusalem. This was not the story of the Good Samaritan, but of the good Jews.

Have you ever had an experience that reminded you of a passage or event in Scripture?

On another day off, an elderly priest, a Lutheran minister, and I decided to walk from Jerusalem to Bethlehem six miles south. When we came in view of the city ahead in the distance, we left the road and made our own path to Bethlehem. Coming upon a Bedouin camp, from our position on a small hill, we noted tents and a sheepfold, as well as at both ends of the camp, large barking dogs. We did not get too close. Continuing our walk, one of us noticed, ahead on a ridge of the hill, a man leading his wife who was riding on a donkey and heading for Bethlehem. I fumbled for my camera but when I looked up, they had vanished over the cusp of the hill. (A photographer once shared with me that some of his best pictures were not in his camera but in his memory. That certainly was my experience. As we approached the spot where we had noticed them, there was no sign of them ahead of us.)

Continuing toward our goal, we came upon a cave and noticed as we entered it, that a small wall separated the front space, where sheep would spend the night, from the inner depths. We also noticed that beyond the wall there was a hole above marked by smoke stains left by a small fireplace located directly below. The scene reminded me of some Christmas representations of the birth of Jesus, which located it not in a stable but in a cave. Indeed, some years later, I discovered a book: *Jesus through Middle Eastern Eyes: Cultural Studies in the Gospels* by Kenneth E. Bailey. In Chapter 1, "The Story of Jesus' Birth: Luke 2:1-20," Bailey argues for Jesus being born in a house rather than a barn or cave:

> . . . simple village homes in Palestine often had two rooms. One was exclusively for guests. That room could be attached to the end of the house or be a 'prophet's chamber' on the roof, as in the story of Elijah (1 Kings 17:19). It was in the main 'family room' that the entire family cooked, ate, slept and lived., while the area next to the door was either a few feet lower than the rest of the floor or blocked off with heavy timbers. Each night into that designated area the family cow, donkey and a few sheep would be driven . . . The farmer *wants* the animals in the house each night because they provide heat in the winter and are safe from theft. This style of traditional home fits naturally into the birth story of Jesus.

Bailey goes on to remark: "The Greek word that is commonly translated "inn" . . . is "simply a place to stay". The same Greek word is used in the preparation for the Passover when Jesus tells his disciples: "The Teacher says to you, where is the *guest room* where I am to eat the

Passover with my disciples?" He goes on to make this distinction: "At his birth the common people sheltered him. The wise men came to the *house*."**64**

It surely seemed to me that the cave experience illustrated an earlier version of the peasant house. Christmas suddenly took on a different meaning for me.

What does this information do to your vision of Christmas?

If you are a photographer, have you ever missed a great photo? Have you identified with this sentiment? "Some of my best photographs are only in my memory, not on film."

What do you make of the fact that the same Greek word is used in the account of Jesus' birth and the celebration of the Last Supper?

Rachel's Tomb, Hebron at the tomb of the patriarchs.

In visiting the location of Rachel's tomb, I experienced a woman talking aloud to Rachel. Later I had this same experience in Hebron at the tomb of the patriarchs. Concerning this tomb, the citing in Wikipedia states:

According to the Book of Genesis Abraham specifically purchased the land for use as a burial plot from Ephron the Hittite, making it one of two purchases by Abraham of real estate in the Land of Canaan, the Promised Land. The book describes how the three patriarchs and their wives, the matriarchs, were buried there. Cenotaphs marked the graves of Abraham and Sarah, Isaac and Rebekah, and Jacob and Leah.

The day we visited this site there was a large group of Jewish people from New York. One man was calling to his wife that the bus was leaving. She replied, "I'm coming, I'm coming, but first I have to finish talking to her".

Are there places of pilgrimage that are part of your life? Have you visited any shrines? What have you taken away from these visits? Is

a walk along the beach a sacred place for you? Would you add other places to your list of sacred places?

Turkey

Visit to Ephesus and Istanbul.

Our visit to Ephesus was memorable on many levels. The archeological work there has discovered and restored a huge dazzling city. The acoustics in the Theatre made a huge impression on us. This was no small park amphitheater; it was huge.

On this visit, however, one point tugged at our heartstrings. A Franciscan priest in residence, amid an overwhelmingly Moslem population, came to supper with us. As he was alone and not part of a Franciscan community, he was eager to share some Christian fellowship. While our meal was not a Eucharist in the strict sense, it was nevertheless, a Christian sharing of breaking bread and conversing. He shared his feeling of isolation. Just what his position was at Ephesus I do not know. However, a place of pilgrimage, the House of the Virgin Mary is there. It is a stone structure based on the belief that Mary; the Mother of Jesus was taken to this house by Saint John. and lived there for the remainder of her earthly life. Popes John Paul II and Benedict XVI visited there.

We also toured Istanbul (formerly Constantinople) and Hagia Sophia. This city was a fascinating place. Many movies have featured it and it is a diverse mixture of people. Hagia Sophia is now a tourist attraction, with a very complex history. The building is gigantic and offers so much to observe and get a feeling for its energy. I regretted that we did not have more time to explore both these places. Ephesus covers such a large area and I would have liked to explore more of it. AT Hagia Sophia my frustration was not having time to pause and meditate and pray.

Have you had the experience of visiting a new place and longing for more time there? Where?

Greece

Athens, Corinth, and Greek islands.

In Greece, we experienced the glory of Athens, the Acropolis over-looking the whole of Athens, the Parthenon dominating the scene, but also the pollution problem attacking many of the ancient treasures. We visited Corinth and viewed the canal hewn out of rock to shorten the trips ships would make to get from the Aegean Sea on the East to the Ionian Sea on the west of Corinth. This canal allowed vessels to avoid the stormy path that the waters to the South of the peninsula often experienced.

On a day off many of us went on a cruise to several islands. The ride on the beautiful waters of the Mediterranean, the restful bathing in the sun, brought out a playful side in most of us as we relaxed.

The study tour ended with us having to write a reflection paper. There was no access to computers available, so my paper consists of eight handwritten pages. It is divided into two sections: 1) Prior Research and 2) The Visit itself. Without sharing the entire paper, here are a few gems.

Research and reading prior to the trip helped to deepen in me a consciousness of the Israelites as a people conditioned in time and space. A growing consciousness of the Jews, not as isolated, but inter-acting with neighbors, conquerors, enemies, has given new form to my understanding of the Scriptures. In the book *Geography of the Bible*, the author speaks about the book and the land. Studying topographical maps helped me to get some idea of the diversity of the land. But what a difference between experiencing the diversity rather than looking at different colorings on maps. Archeological sites highlighted the inter-action between the Israelites and the Canaanites and how this is present in the Scriptures. Since archaeologists have a specialized vocabulary, becoming familiar with this, allowed me to listen better to people in the field. Somehow or other, the notion of Jewish history continuing after Christ, never struck home to me. The Jewish holy cities of Safad, Tiberias, and Hebron were now added to the Holy City of Jerusalem.

The visit itself gave me significant new insights. A certain sense of one civilization literally building upon another came home with remarkable clarity at the tells. How many times did we not hear some listing of levels upon levels—Canaanite shrine, Israel holy place, synagogue, Byzantine Church, Crusader Church, mosque. A special experience for me was visiting the Canaanite site of worship under the Church of the Transfiguration at Mt. Tabor. Somehow the sense and primitive state of the Canaanite and Israelite worship prior to the Solomonic temple gave great meaning to me for understanding parts of the Pentateuch. These types of demythologizing have been helpful to me. From visits and lectures I learned that biblical research and archeology are truly dynamic. The land and the people have impressed me much more powerfully than many holy places. My walk from Jerusalem to Bethlehem gave me a much better sense of distances.

Let me conclude by giving several instances of things and scriptural passages which I have captured in picture and understanding. My final hope is that the present insights are but a foretaste of what reading and praying the Scriptures will hold for me. If this be true the experience of the sites, sounds, smells, tastes and feel will be a present part of my life.

We left Athens by plane to return to New York.

Can you recall an experience in your life, which exposed you to a great bit of history and culture? When and Where?

(My scripture knowledge became exponentially increased because of this journey. Moreover, I took a great number of pictures that I transitioned to slides, which I have used often in Scripture presentations. Four years later when I was applying for the M.A. program in Scripture at Catholic Theological Union in Chicago, four credits based on this this trip were accepted as fulfillment toward the degree.)

2. <u>MEXICO, NICARAGUA, ECUADOR, PERU.</u>

Mexico

While I was studying for the M.A. in Scripture, my dear friend Bob Bossie shared with me that a priest he worked with at the Eighth Day Center for Peace and Justice in Chicago had led him and others on a trip to South America where he said he began to read the scriptures from the bottom up. I do not think I ever asked him what precisely he meant by that. However, my own experience was to see how ordinary peasants gathered in Basic Christian Communities to share, discuss, and apply the Scriptures to their living. They did not rely on Scripture scholars.

Shortly after, I learned that Chuck Dahm, OP, was organizing another trip--would I be interested. I was available during the summer of my two-year stay in Chicago. Thus, in summer of 1981, I journeyed with this unbelievable guide to Mexico, Nicaragua, Ecuador, and Peru.

We left Chicago and flew to Mexico City, where the ride from the airport to our place of residence for the next two weeks began a process of enculturation. One of Chuck's fellow Dominicans was studying in Mexico City at the time and had arranged for places to visit and speakers to educate us.

Our first presentation was at the Center of Theological Reflection, the base from which we would operate. Our first speaker made us aware that Mexico is a reality different from Central and South America. Our continuing trip to Nicaragua, Ecuador, and Peru would flesh out this awareness. Heading home after our first day, a bit of exploration of Mexico City, we boarded a public bus, providing us another cultural difference. People entered the rear door and passed their money up to the driver. Charlie said, "Can you imagine that in Chicago?"

Have you had an event in your life that made you aware of cultural differences? If so, what was the experience?

On our second day we learned much more from several present-ers. Marcos Viallman a professor of history offered an analysis of the economic and political history of Latin America, Central America, and the Caribbean. One member of our group was Art McGovern, a Jesuit professor at Detroit University who had published *Marxism: An American Christian Perspective*. He described the presentation as a very sophisticated Marxist analysis.

Changing focus, Luis de Valle, one of the creative Mexican Liberation Theologians, spoke about the Reign of God, the church, and relations of local churches to Basic Christian Communities. Jesuit teams and seminars, for example, were some groups formed for such reflection. I asked what scriptures are important for this work. He responded, "The prophets and the Gospels."

Later our experiences with various *Communidades de Base* ampli-fied the information received in these presentations.

In your life, have you had the experience of listening to a lecture giving theory on a topic and then followed by an existential experi-ence? If so, what kinds of reflections would you have on the difference between the two experiences?

A visit to Cuernavaca was also on our schedule. There at the ca-thedral, we met Bishop Sergio Mendez Arceo, who informed us that he had studied history but now his call was to *make* history. At Vatican II, he provided the most interventions by a Latin American bishop. A supporter of Socialism he visited Cuba and Nicaragua to learn from their governing experiences. We saw protest signs against the bishop in various parts of Mexico calling him a Communist. In actuality he was a solid supporter of Basic Christian Communities, *Comunidades de Base*. Most of us on this trip had some vague ideas of what *a Communidad de Base* was, but we would learn, by visiting them, what they were, and how they functioned.

Are you familiar with the term Basic Christian Communities? What does it mean to you?

On the weekend, our group dispersed two by two to different areas of Mexico. Charles Brown and I were to bus to Tehuantepec. However, we would not leave till 4:00 P. M. so we explored a couple of churches on our way back from the post office, both staffed by religious order priests who told us Bishop Mendez wasn't too popular with other Mexican bishops. Another of their views was that Nicaragua is under the influence of Cuba and Cuba is under Russia. Since Nicaragua was on our agenda, we took this forewarning under advisement. (Fortunately, we learned from our experience that the reality there was quite different from that in Cuba.)

Our bus ride south lasted from 5:00 P.M. until 6:00 A. M. We went through Puebla at night and passed a large Volkswagen factory, eventually we stopped to transfer to a different bus, then to yet another for the last leg of our journey, or so we thought.

Finally, in Tehuantepec we attended a Zone meeting with the priests and sisters of five parishes. The bishop was in jeans and a T-shirt, with a little wooden cross around his neck. Just as Bishop Mendez Arceo, had done, he asked us each to first introduce ourselves and when the meeting was over, we ate and left promptly by car, then bus, arriving at our next stop for the Saturday night Mass. As confessions were going on, Fr. Joe invited us to nap a while on cots in the sacristy and eventually he led us by flashlight to the Jesuit house where we were met by the guard dog. Fr. Jose opened the shutters and a cloud of mosquitoes greeted us. When they cleared, he showed us the shower, located in a separate building. (A heating coil wrapped around the waterspout provided the hot water.) Supper was next: shrimp, tortillas, mangos and soup, the usual meal of the people living so close to the coast. The house was simple-- everything up on blocks, and, inside, four beds and mosquito netting. After some instruction about the need to make sure mosquitoes did not get under the netting, we had an interesting conversation during which Fr.

explained the option for the poor that the Jesuits had made which had brought him to this parish.

This experience reminded me that I had joined the Priests of the Sacred Heart with the desire to be a foreign missionary. It also made me wonder whether I would have what was needed to live as these Jesuit missionaries were living. How about you-- ever have an experience like this where you might not have known what you were asking for?

The next day Charlie and I accompanied Fr. Roberto to a different church of the parish, while another team, Fr. Carlos and Vera, went to the train to head for missions more distant. Upon arrival at our destination, where it was First Communion day, Roberto first heard confessions and then invited me to concelebrate the Mass that followed. Roberto had lots of interaction with the children, and after his brief homily, he invited others to speak. Six people responded. At the Canon, he asked me to pray a part and as the Mass concluded, Roberto invited me to offer a brief message. In my halting Spanish, I said: *"Estas palabras son muy importante por mi, Cuerpo de Cristo, y iglesia. Muchas gracias. Yo me gusto mucho aqui."* ("These words are very important to me, Body of Christ and Church. Many thanks. I like it here very much.") Roberto joked with the congregation that the Holy Spirit had come upon me. (I did not know much Spanish in 1981.) After this he made some announcements about the work on the new church building and then stressed to the congregation: "You the people are the Church." After sharing a meal with the principal of the local school and the first communicants we returned to the priests' house for more conversation with Jose, Luis and Roberto. However, Roberto excused himself to head to Mexico City.

This was a quite different experience of church that made me wish I knew more Spanish, but it was joyful even without my knowing the language. Ever have a similar experience?

In the morning we attended the funeral of a woman who had died during an abortion. Today was the funeral. Black was the color of the day and questioned the competency of the female doctor.

Charlie who had accompanied one of the other priests to a peninsula gathering, arrived back and we prepared for our return to Mexico City. This trip proved to be eventful. We made the first stop and waited from 2:00 until 8:00 but still missed our bus and had to hustle to change the tickets. On the bus there was a bathroom in the back, right behind us, its stink combined with that of the diesel. We had a choice" open the window and freeze or keep it closed and die of asphyxiation. We chose the former for this twelve-hour ride. Finally, back in Mexico City we took the packed Metro, eventually arriving at the retreat house, where we were happy to shower, shave, and sleep.

Talk about an immersion experience! This trip was certainly one. We experienced cultural differences and shared community reflection on our experiences and those of the tour group. Do you take the opportunity to reflect on various experiences? Have you ever been part of a consciousness-raising trip, which included community reflection? Would you like to have such an experience?

With no scheduled activities the next day, I took advantage of this opportunity to explore the shrine of Our Lady of Guadalupe despite being visited by Montezuma's revenge. We were also able to make a visit to the Pyramids. After time spent there, we headed downtown to the Cathedral where it almost felt like walking into another era. We visited the city museum where there are wonderful and powerful murals and models of what an Aztec city would have looked like. The layers of one building on another are everywhere.

The following morning, we visited with a Basic Christian community on the periphery of Mexico City. Bishop Arceo Mendez had introduced us to these groups, formed around hearing the Word of God, reflecting on it for their personal and communal lives and then deciding on action At Mass we were introduced to a 73-year-old woman, a catechist accepted as the priest of the parish. The prayers of the faithful included petitions for El Salvador, its people, and their problems in the Colonias, such as violence, hunger, drainage and with a multiplicity of other issues.

We learned that the Jesuits had decided that their theory of educating the wealthy was not working. Their involvement in high schools and colleges was based on the belief that if they educated students to the Church's call to work for justice, they could change the conditions of injustice and inequality. Therefore, they took the radical step, closed their high schools and colleges, and moved toward working with Basic Christian communities. The theology of the Jesuit students met the reality of the poor and experienced the See, Judge, and Act methodology.

As a member of the Priests of the Sacred Heart I found myself reflecting on the emphasis of the Development Offices of my community in the United States. Devotion to the Sacred Heart was the main focus. For some time, my thinking was that there is need to be involved with the social doctrine of the Church. I shared my thoughts with one of the Jesuits. His reply seemed right on the mark: "But people will stop supporting you".

What do you think about the "option for the poor" that the Jesuits in Mexico made? What do you make of the response of the Jesuit, "But people will stop supporting you"? Would you agree with him? Why or why not?

Near the end of our time in Mexico, we were off to an information center. Here the people who compile info take it for granted that United Press International (UPI) and Associated Press (AP) support the multi-nationals. They spoke about programs of formation for religious, and of a project underway to re-write history from the underside, the view of the conquered. We heard from a man connected with Guatemala who told of the horrific atrocities taking place there.

The casualness with which the presenters spoke about the support for the multi-nationals was a bit jolting. Their perspective would be affirmed repeatedly on this trip. How about you? Have you ever been surprised when a different perspective is presented casually which may challenge your own? If so; when and about what?

> At this point I hope you have acquired a general sense of the format our days followed. Rather than continue in this style, instead of giving a day by day account, I will highlight particular experiences for your consideration.

Nicaragua

The flight from Mexico City to Nicaragua made a stop in San Salvador, El Salvador, where. I experienced a kind of ominous feeling. There were few people around. Only a reporter for the New York Times got off. Nobody got on. On both sides of the plane, armed soldiers monitored the luggage. As the plane took off, my feelings relaxed as the green hills looked beautiful below. What will become of this country?

As I write this today, (March 20, 2019) great numbers of families from El Salvador are crossing the border of the U.S. from Mexico. President Trump has declared an emergency at the border to gain funds for his "wall". For us who live in the Rio Grande Valley of Texas, and for other concerned citizens, the emergency is the present administration's horrific mistreatment of these refugees fleeing violence and death and seeking asylum in the U.S.

What have you heard about the Southern Border of the United States? How much do you know of the issue of immigration, not only in the U.S. but also in other parts of the world?

On arrival I was struck by the almost jubilant greeting we received, reflecting a huge disconnect between what we had heard in the States and what the people expressed to us. On our first night in our residence, which was a formation house for candidates hoping to join a religious order, the director explained to us the change from working with the rich to working with the poor. We had heard this theme from the Jesuits in Mexico and now locals repeated it here in Nicaragua.

Working with the rich meant teaching them the Catholic Tradition of Social Action. The hope was that they would incorporate this into their personal and communal lives. This vision proved to be an illusion. Head knowledge did not lead to action, it was theoretical not practical.

The option for the poor means presence with them and seeing them as the agents of change. People gather in Basic Christian Communities where they listen to the scriptures, discusses their meaning, and then apply them to their life and community. Thus, from prayer, reflection, and discernment come strategies for action.

In Mexico, we had heard of the U.S. perception of affairs in Mexico and further south. Now our experience brought a completely different perspective.

Have certain experiences in your life altered or destroyed previous perceptions? If so, when and how?

The role of the United States in the country of Nicaragua was and is complicated and contentious. Today in 2019, Daniel Ortega is president for the second time. (Whatever the reason the number of refugees from Nicaragua coming to the United States is not as many as those coming from the Central American Northern Triangle: Honduras, Guatemala, and El Salvador.)

Early in our visit, we kept hearing "Somocista" and "Sandinista." Learning the meaning of these terms and abbreviations, which used the first letter of a number of words, were only the beginning of what would be a continuing endeavor for us.

We learned that the first term referred to the followers of Anastasio "Tachito" Somoza DeBayle. He was president of Nicaragua twice. However, as dictator, head of the National Guard, he was the de facto ruler of the country from 1967 to 1979. He was the last member of the Somoza family to be president, ending a dynasty that had been in power since 1936.

The second term referred to the members of the revolutionary party, who took their name from Sandino who led the defeat of the US Marines who occupied the country from 1909 to 1933 The letters FSLN identify this party, *Frente Sandinista de Liberacion Nacional* (Sandinista National Liberation Front.) Both Somoza and Sandino died by assassination.

The Wikipedia article on Daniel Ortega illustrates one aspect of the contention between the U.S. and Nicaragua:

In1981, United States President Ronald Reagan accused the FSLN of joining with Soviet-backed Cuba in supporting Marxist revolutionary movements in other Latin American countries such as El Salvador. People within the Reagan administration authorized the Central Intelligence Agency to begin financing, arming, and training rebels, some of whom were former officers from Somoza's National Guard, as anti-Sandinista guerrillas who were known collectively as the Contras. This also led to one of the largest political scandals in US history, (the Iran–Contra affair), when Oliver North and several members of the Reagan administration defied the Boland Amendment, selling arms to Iran and then using the proceeds to fund the Contras. The Contra war would claim 30,000 lives.

Four years later, this contention surfaced in a new way. President Reagan described Daniel Ortega as a "dictator in designer glasses" while accusing the Sandinistas of using Cuban aid combined with terrorists to turn their country into a breeding ground for subversion. Then, as now, history was too easily forgotten.

Daniel Ortega, however, did not disappear. He resurfaced in the 1984 general election and won the presidency. In 1990, he lost but ran again in 1996 and 2001, and lost both times. However, he ran in 2006 and won for the second time. He continues as president to the present.

The initial process of getting a feel for terminology led to many detailed and interesting presentations for us on the history and reality in Nicaragua. Our trip was in the summer of 1981 prior to the Reagan-Ortega conflict, which took place in December. The experience we had surely gave a very different understanding to this contention and events that followed.

In the States, many people equated the Cuban revolution and the Nicaraguan revolution. Here people explained the many differences. The role of the Catholic Church in these two revolutions was very different. In Cuba, the Church allied with the rich. In Nicaragua the Church split in allegiance, some allied with the rich, but a significant number of clergy and communities allied with the poor and were members of Basic Christian Communities and organizing.

After the victory of the Sandinistas, the new government appointed several priests to positions in the government. Fernando Cardenal, S.J. who organized the national literacy program, told us that when he was teaching in the University about Plato and Aristotle, he had twenty students. This the bishops did not mind. But now that he was involved in political formation and had about sixty students, this was a problem. He was one of the coordinating committee "12" and an important figure in the early days. He was in charge of the literacy campaign and the work of Pablo Freire in connecting literacy and democracy influenced him. Students from Cuba helped him. People were seeking to understand their own values as opposed to accepting the values imposed on them. Fernando's brother, Ernesto Cardenal, was better known because of the picture of John Paul II, on his visit to Nicaragua, pointing his figure at the kneeling priest. He also was somewhat known for the *Gospel of Solentiname*, a four-volume set of a community's reflections on the Gospels. Ernesto was a member of this community.

Miguel D'Escoto of Maryknoll, foreign minister in the Nicaraguan government after the revolution, spoke to us for two and a half hours about the history of the country. Prior to this, he had founded Orbis

Books and in his senior years became president of the U.N. General Assembly.

We met a woman who was broken hearted over the developments in Chile. She shared that she had to have keys for five different houses to avoid the police state. Amid this turmoil, she struggled with pacifism. Pictures of Sr. Maura and Sr. Ita who were raped and murdered in El Salvador hung on the walls of the home of Peggy Healey, a Maryknoll sister and friend. They inspired her to continue her work in Nicaragua. Fr. Uriel, a Franciscan priest scripture scholar, shared with us his personal struggle and prayerful discernment needed to come to the choice for the Sandinistas.

One of the challenging aspects of this tour was being open to the different perspectives of Mexicans and Central and South Americans. The popular understanding in the U.S. of many aspects of these countries and the history of U.S. interventions is often very much mistaken.

What we see on MSNBC and Fox News illustrates different perspectives and analyses. Print media and radio stations also have very different perspectives. What is the source of your news? Where do you get your news?

Have you ever had a personal struggle, like Fr. Uriel and the Chilean woman, and turned to prayerful discernment to make a choice?

Ecuador

Our flight from Nicaragua stopped in San Jose, Costa Rica, then on to Panama. We spent the night in the airport then flew to Quito, a city in the Mountains that offers some beautiful views. We headed east and made stops in Otavalo and an indigenous center at Ambato. The next leg of the trip to Puyo was by bus. The narrow road hugged the side of a mountain above a river below. The drop off was scary but somehow the driver navigated its blind curves. I do not quite recall how those approaching from different directions would signal so as not to have a head- on collision on one of the curves. However, we made it to Puyo.

There we met with a bishop of the Dominican order who told us about his few priests and their pastoral work. We also learned that the river was a tributary to the Amazon.

Have you ever had an experience, which raised your anxiety as this bus ride did for me?

Our next surprise came in the form of news that there was going to be a bus strike. Not knowing how long such a strike would last, we immediately headed off back across Ecuador to the Peruvian border. Then another surprise: we learned that Peru was observing a holiday and there would be no bus transportation. We spent the day in the bus station at the border town of Tumbe and when the buses resumed service, we headed for an overnight trip to the coastal town of Chimbote.

Most of us have heard or used the expression: "When it rains it pours." This part of our travel was a classic example of the unexpected surprise phenomenon. Have you had a similar experience? What emotions did you feel? How did it end?

Peru

In Chimbote, we received an explanation of the term "Popular Religion". Three aspects of poor people's faith, which have a liberating dynamic, are notable:

1. Prayer: ministry is not only to be nourished by it in process but begin with it. The poor have wisdom, logic different from many rich. They trust in God as a liberating power. The same goes for the Saints. Their prayer is like the psalms. They get angry, demand from God, and punish the Saints.

2. Fiesta: this event takes place in most communities for a week, is a time for joy and rejoicing. RECIPROCITY is the most important characteristic of Andean culture—mutual service. The people have a symbolic language expressed in dance and other

art. One person expressed the meaning of Fiesta this way: "we are protesting against a technical way of life".

3. Insight of Justice: Mutual love does not accept mistreatment of others. There is a cult of "mother earth"*Pacha mama.*

In a recent trip to Cusco, Willka Tika, and Machu Pichu, we witnessed people living out of their indigenous religious roots in several religious services conducted by native Quechua shamans. They invited us to participate and we did. Our guide shared his journey with us from Catholicism to his indigenous roots and practices. In other words, we experienced "Popular religion" in a lived experience. We experienced reciprocity, shared community care for one another, and reverence for nature and *Pacha mama.*

We carried with us our consciousness of "Climate Change" and people's reaction to it. The Andean people have much to teach us on this topic. What is your attitude regarding climate change? Have you adapted behaviors, which show your consciousness and efforts to save our Earth?

Our journey took us along the Pan American Highway to Lima, where Fr. Jeff Kleiber, SJ. offered us a historical perspective on Peru with particular focus on the Catholic Church. Because it was quite detailed and complicated, I took extensive notes. The Peruvian Church consists of divisions, reflected in the hierarchy and clergy. Fr. Kleiber's information often contrasted the history of Peru with that of other countries in South and Central America. Despite many similarities, there were also some very significant differences. We were in Lima for six days and visited a wide variety of people and places including the convent of St. Rose of Lima and the house where St. Martin de Porres lived and ministered. It is quite fitting that now it is a location serving the disabled.

My personal experience has been that many, if not most, people in the United States know very little or nothing about South American history. Prior to this trip, that was true of me. As we listened and learned it became more and more real for me that this was a "consciousness raising" experience. I determined that my future focus would be the countries of America to the South of the United States.

As I am writing this, living in proximity to the Southern Border of the U.S. with Mexico, people from Guatemala, El Salvador, and Honduras are arriving in great numbers at our border. The history of these countries and U.S. involvement has created the conditions, which are driving these refugees north. What is your perspective on the present phenomenon?

On July 27, we flew from Lima to Cusco. The change in altitude was of concern. Many people suffer considerably from "altitude sickness" which is accompanied by headaches, vomiting and cramps. Sister Sue, a friend, who had been living and ministering in Lima for several years, encouraged me to drink the Coca Tea. I did so and had only minimal negative effects from the altitude.

The plaza in Cusco was a fascinating mix of indigenous groups playing their music with a great variety of flutes, guitars, and drums and other instruments. There were many vendors and quite a number of tourists. After lodging for the night in a Dominican convent, the next day we left by train for Machu Pichu, where it immediately became obvious why this place is on many people's bucket lists. Its history, architecture, and design tend to be overwhelming. One would never have enough time to explore it. Upon leaving Cusco we journeyed first by train and then by bus to Sicuani. The bus broke down and Chuck Dahm had to hail a variety of trucks to carry us to our destination. Here we got a lesson in language ability when we met two men vendors who spoke Spanish, Quechua, and Aymara. They were selling large pots for grain.

On arrival to our destination, we met and shared with the Carmelite bishop, Tony Quinn and learned about the radio ministry, an important part of their missionary efforts. We also heard there of a negative attitude toward popular religiosity, which was very different from what we had heard in Chimbote. Opus Dei came under heavy criticism as did the various sects, which preach a "God and me" religion, totally neglecting the need for involvement to change oppressive conditions.

Our next adventure was at Lake Titicaca where we travelled by small boats to the various islands and discovered a different lifestyle from anything we had seen previously.

This leg of our journey exposed us to the different attitudes and ministries taking place in Peru. It certainly was a cautionary tale not to generalize. Travel is an education. Have you been influenced by travel? If so how?

At the end of the trip, I stayed for another week in Callao, the port city of Lima, with a friend, an Ursuline sister from Kentucky.

Before leaving Peru, I heard these wise words from my friend Sr. Mary Sue: "When we find ourselves, we have new life to lose for others." "Don't idealize the poor as there are liars and thieves among them as well."

PERU, BRAZIL. 1987

Return to Peru

I had been to Peru in 1981, but this time I was going to visit Sr. Mary Sue who was now up in the mountain area San Miguel de Pallaques, a town in northern Peru, the capital of San Miguel Province in Cajamarca Region. Getting there entailed catching a bus in Lima, which took the Pan American Highway north passing through Chimbote and Trujillo. I went to sleep and was startled by shouts *"Chilete, Chilete"*. which I knew was where I needed to get off the bus. We arrived at 5:15 A. M. in total dark and I had no idea where to go next. By 6:00, the first dawn of day crept over the hills—the sun not appearing until about 8:45. I observed a lot going on-- market, schoolchildren in uniforms trekking here and there, and time seemed to pass quite quickly but no Sue. Luckily, there was much activity to occupy me. However, eventually some anxiety began to arise. Finally, Sue arrived at noon. We boarded a small truck (*camioneta*) and headed out of town toward more hills, riding in the back of the vehicle. At a juncture in the road, we changed to a different truck and changed our seating, now were riding in the cab heading to San Miguel. Sue conversed with the driver while I took in the marvelous scenery as we continued going up and up, arriving at 5:00.

I was having an awesome beginning to this visit. However, it was a mixture of excitement and anxiety.

Have you experienced excitement and anxiety at the same time?

I had not looked at this journal for many years, and now I was astounded to read the sixteen pages covering that time in Peru. Some highlights: San Miguel has a large white church, thanks to the contribution of people from Lima who once lived here. Sue and another sister, who live in a little balcony apartment-like section of the sacristy, interact in so many ways with the people. One of the parishioners told me she likes the preaching of the sisters better than that of the visiting priest who comes at various times.

(I too have been discouraged by the lack of good preaching by priests. This parishioner's experience rang true to me. So now I follow a great web site, Catholic Women Preach.)

On my second day, before sunrise, I accompanied Sue, riding on a milk truck for an hour and a half to get to Llappa and passing through beautiful agricultural scenes. While Sue prepared for her class, I napped. First shooting stars entertained me, nice for preparing for sleep! Later while she was in class, I began to wander and came upon four young men mixing plaster, hauling buckets up a rustic ladder to the man who was applying it to the walls. When they invited me to climb the ladder, without hesitation, I followed them up to the second level. They paused from their labor; one took a swig from a bottle and handed it to the next worker who did the same then passed the bottle to me. I took a swig and discovered what "fire water" tastes like. All this happened with my primitive knowledge of Spanish.

I was to find out that this custom of "toasting" and then sharing was part of the culture. Are there some cultural customs in your family?

After returning to San Miguel I attended a baptism and the reception that followed and included more drinking. The father offered a toast and drank from a glass. He passed the bottle and glass to the next man and the process proceeded. I was included.

I visited a variety of people and had wonderful conversations on life in Peru and international happenings and after my weeklong stay I returned to Lima. When I got to the airport, I was surprised to notice that right next to the plane for my next flight was one from the Russian airline, Aeroflot. I do not believe I had ever seen an Aeroflot plane in a U.S. airport. My next flight went over La Paz and Lake Titicaca and after a stop in Rio, on to Sao Paulo.

Brazil

In Sao Paulo I was met at the airport by Jose Fernandez Oliveira, SCJ, with whom I studied at Sacred Heart Monastery in Hales Corners, Wisconsin. I spent the night in an SCJ house. We left the next day for Taubate, the location of the theological school of the two Brazilian provinces of the Priests of the Sacred Heart, located midway between the main cities Sao Paulo and Rio and a perfect place for the conference. Along with two others from the U.S., we gathered for an educational experience arranged by the SCJ headquarters in Rome. There were missionaries from Africa, Mozambique, Holland, Belgium, Italy, North Brazilian province, Germany, Cameroon, and other countries as well. There were also representatives from the Provincial Councils and General Council. This was to be a month of presentations, group discussions, and field trips. Portuguese, French, and English were the languages for three different groupings.

The size and diversity of Brazil impressed all of us who were first time visitors, as did the Brazilian Church which has had a bi-annual plan for many years. The Brazilian bishops were part of several important National gatherings of bishops: In 1953 the National Bishops Conference was established, In 1968 Medellin proclaimed the "Option for the poor", In 1978 Puebla affirmed and expanded Medellin.

. The Catholic Worker method of See, Judge, and Act is widespread in Brazil. We were privileged to have a session with Cardinal Arns, a great promoter of Basic Christian Communities. The pastoral works of the South Brazilian province are quite varied. The SCJs are in charge of the St. Jude Shrine, which is a place of prayer, pilgrimage, and local pastoral work. We also visited parishes ranging from middle class to *favelas*. Frei Beto, a important liberation theologian, gave an interesting talk on method. He is a somewhat controversial figure, it seems, because of his openness to learn from Communist analysis, and contact with Cuba.

Several processes sought input from us. One exercise was on values. We were asked to list the ten main values we see in the U.S., then to list our ten personal values and finally what we perceived to be the ten top values in Brazil. The methodology consisted of small language groups then large General Sessions in which the small groups shared results. Daily Mass and a day of Recollection were part of the experience.

I have two notebooks from this conference. One contains fifty pages of information presented by speakers, the other is twelve pages of my own reflections.

But the Brazilian experience wasn't all intellectual. We visited the famous shrine venerating the Blessed Virgin at Aparecida and the famous recreation beach of Copacabana. We toured Rio de Janeiro and the route of the Mardi Gras, took a cable car up to Sugar Loaf Mountain, and by cab visited the statue *of Cristo Redentor*. We also visited a barrio parish staffed by Brazilian SCJs. The youth involvement was large and very active.

The international aspect of my Brazil experience was new for me and very enriching. I was surprised that I could understand so much of the French. Though my Spanish was not very developed yet, I could communicate with those who spoke Spanish, Italian, and Portuguese and was pleasantly surprised to be able to understand the Portuguese newspapers.

Travel has been an education for me in various aspects of geography and customs. The Brazil trip included interaction with the international aspect of the Priests of the Sacred Heart, a variety of languages, and highly enlightening experiences of the participants.

In your own experiences, can you relate to mine?

EL SALVADOR, NICARAGUA, AND GUATEMALA. July 1988.

The itinerary for this trip was a full three pages. We met with political and religious leaders. Here I will simply write about the events that most affected my perceptions. My Journal for this trip is forty-eight pages.

El Salvador

Our meeting on the first day was with the Vice Minister of Social Development, Ministry of the Interior, Lic. Miriam Trejo de Portillo. She gave a broad presentation, but what struck me the most was learning that 20,000 Salvadoran people living in Houston send a great sum of money back to El Salvador. This contribution is an important part of the country's economy. Next, we visited the Cathedral where Archbishop (now Saint) Oscar Romero is buried. At the time, his tomb was a plain simple affair. Since then it has become more ostentatious. As he now has been declared a Saint, I wonder what will happen with his tomb.

We also met with the Mothers of the Disappeared and an American journalist with the *Christian Science Monitor*.

On our second morning we arrived at 10:00 for a political briefing at the forbidding U.S. embassy. The physical aspect of the embassy has stuck with me more than the "information" we received. As we arrived, we saw barbed wire, machine gun bunkers, and metal detectors. At this time, the U.S. was providing $1,000,000 a day to the Salvadoran government. How strange it seemed to need this elaborate protection. First, as we approached a Salvadoran soldier had to clear us. We then passed through a metal detector manned by a U.S. Marine and finally entered a bunker to hear the U.S. government's take on the existing reality. The information communicated at the early presentation by government officials would later be contradicted by information we received from contact with local citizens of San Salvador, El Salvador.

In U.S. Embassies, the officials communicated a consistent pattern of discrepancy and deception, which did not match the reality we experienced. Though proud to be a United States citizen, I experienced shame at many of the policies of the U.S. in Mexico, Central America and South America.

Do you have any or much knowledge about U.S. involvement in other countries? What are your perceptions?

In the evening at 5:30, we were blessed to meet with the scholarly, humble, and caring Father Jon Sobrino, .SJ. who was in Thailand when a government death squad murdered his fellow Jesuits, their housekeeper and her daughter.

This is how he structured his talk: 1) My view of the country, 2) What happened when the poor organized for life, 3) El Salvador a reality of poor and crucified people vs. being ignored, distorted. For me the man was the message, and I especially remember his statement: "We live in a world of death which gives death and tries to lie about it." Yet he found hope in the people's creativity and community. I also remember one of the participant's observation: "Before we were told that Jesus died for the truth, and now we are told that Jesus died for the truth and justice." One person stated, "Bishop Oscar Romero said very bluntly to the rich: 'Take the rings off your fingers before they cut your hand off'".

We spent our last full day in the countryside. While we visited this very poor community living on corn that they grew, a group of armed men (not sure if there were women as well) suddenly emerged (from I know not where) and calmly passed by us. One of the community leaders said *"estos muchachos estan luchando por nuestra pais"* These young people are struggling for our country. At the U.S. embassy, they would be described as guerillas.

The words "fake news" have come to dominate much analysis and commentary in the U.S. during the first term of President Trump. Do you feel you have been deceived by "fake news"? If you are on Facebook, do you believe some of the posts you read are fake?

Nicaragua

The next day we moved on to Nicaragua, where I had visited in 1981. We heard talks on the economy, visited a textile factory, got an update on the literacy campaign, and learned about the agrarian reform. We visited with those wounded in the war for liberation, as well as with mothers who had lost their sons, and met with officials at the U.S Embassy. Again, we experienced a great dissonance in what we heard from these officials and from people in the various communities.

The struggle between the government and the Church continues, as does the involvement of the Nicaraguan government with other suffering countries.

Guatemala

Ending our trip in Guatemala, we visited an Indigenous community where only five men lived with a population of women and children. The other men had been killed in the genocide which the government was pursuing. Our guides told us not to take any pictures or publicize them because it would endanger the people. We learned about the specialness of Guatemalan weaving which identified people's geographical location by colors and designs. Two women accompanied us to translate from the local language to Spanish, which then our guide translated from

Spanish to English for our group. We were intrigued by learning of the Heifer project, working to end hunger and poverty, the organization donated a pair of goats to this community. At night, they place the goats into elevated cages with slats at the bottom so that the farmers can easily collect their droppings and then use them to fertilize the crops. When the goats produce new arrivals, they are fed to breeding age and then passed on to a separate community to begin the process all over. A helping organization in Germany had enabled the community to dig a well and provide a safe water supply. This hard-working group provided us with a meal and wonderful hospitality.

Have you ever had the experience of visiting a community with such scarce resources? Have you experienced tremendous hospitality from a poor community or a poor person?

For me our visit to the Market in Chichicastenango was very special. Booths were everywhere. I had brought with me a special stole which I received from a missionary who had worked in Guatemala, and I wanted to purchase another. The market was a maze of booths. How would I ever find what I was looking for? I do not remember if I tried my limited Spanish or someone helped me, but I got detailed instructions on how to find my way: "You follow this aisle and go past four aisles that go off to your left; at the fifth aisle you go right and you will find your booth at the fourth booth on the left". I decided to test my faith and surge ahead. My faith was rewarded, and I arrived through the maze to the correct booth. I had made it! *Que milagro!* In addition, I purchased several stoles.

Another aspect of this visit to Chichicastenango involved religious themes. Outside the Catholic Church, shamans were using incense and leading prayer chants. Inside there were the usual statues of Catholic saints but also the incense and chants. We seemed to be experiencing some kind of mix of very different religious experiences.

Our visit to Guatemala ended with a chance to hear and ask questions of Bishop Juan Gerardi, director of the Guatemalan Truth Commission. Again, for me the Man was the message, even though there was so much information in his sharing. Sometime later I was saddened to learn that an assailant had murdered him for his work for justice.

Summarizing this trip, I would say I experienced contact with saints: Rutilio Grande, SJ., Oscar Romero, the Mothers of the killed or disappeared, Jon Sobrino, SJ, and Bishop Juan Gerardi.

Have you had an experience where you reflected afterwards, "I have been in the presence of a Saint"? If so, when and with whom?

I see that my listing is heavily saturated with bishops and priests. When I made most of these trips south, I did not know much Spanish. Therefore, I depended on translation to get a sense of what many were sharing. It would be different now. With my fluency in Spanish I could have direct contact and not have to learn second hand from people. Even with this limitation I was greatly enriched by these experiences.

Chapter Seven

Spiritual experiences.

1) RETREAT AT BETHANY SPRING NEW HAVEN, KENTUCKY. VISIT TO GETHSEMANE AND THOMAS MERTON'S HERMITAGE. MAY 23, 1988

IN MAY 1988, I WAS in a period of transition. Many years previously, I had visited Gethsemane in Kentucky, but now I had discovered that there was a retreat house offering directed retreats a short distance from there.

The first passage from Scripture that Sister Janice, my director, pointed me to was Jeremiah 29:11-14. Vs. 11: "For I know well the plans I have in mind for you, plans for your welfare and not for woe, so as to give you a future of hope." Vs. 14: "I will gather you from . . . . . . all the places where I have dispersed you—it is Yahweh who speaks".

My notes: "God I've felt dispersed. Guess the dispersion did not seem to feel like from you. I have learned self-defeating behaviors, family patterns of withdrawal, silence, separation. The dispersion felt like depression & separation from you . . . My prayer of Lent two years ago: "Grant me a steadfast spirit of fervor". This Lent you seemed to have gathered me together."

This first experience confirmed that Jesus was gardening me. My journaling, on the passages that my director chose for me, go on for twenty-four pages. Jeremiah has always attracted me, with his boldness in communicating with God. I found some of this boldness in my prayer time. Scripture passages drew forth memories from the past. I expressed myself in words in my journal but also in poetry and artistic representations. Much imagery from the Litany of the Sacred Heart came alive for me. All these realities were confirmation that Jesus was directing (gardening) me.

Have you ever made a directed retreat? Can you recall times in your life when you had the assurance that what was happening was the work of Jesus, the Holy Spirit, guiding and inspiring? If so, when?

Being this close to the Monastic home of Thomas Merton, I began reading *The Seven Mountains of Thomas Merton* by Michael Mott. When I learned of his hermitage, I wanted to visit it. Sister Janice gave me directions on how to reach it and avoid the main gate. I succeeded, and took several pictures, but, curiously, as I look at my notes, I realize I did not write anything about my visit there. The information in Mott's book about meetings Merton had with prominent people, at a lake across the street from the Abbey sparked my curiosity to visit that spot. For me these were truly meditative moments.

I also visited Merton's grave, which, paradoxically, was right next to that of the Abbot with whom he had many difficulties. Mott's book was a map for me. It showed me what to look for at the Abbey of Gethsemane. Liturgy in the chapel with the monks was a gift and their chant engaging and inspiring.

My friend Fr. Sebastian Muccilli was a great admirer of Merton and conversations with him had educated me a bit about the influence Merton had on spirituality.

My own thoughts were directed to examining how the many experiences of my trips in the third world and beyond have influenced my own spirituality. The open question for me now was "What does this mean for me in my continuing journey?"

Can you recall in your life when you felt directed to something in the future, but you were not sure how that would develop? What happened?

My next adventure flowed from some of my reflections during the directed retreat. I did not have to wait long to feel the direction Jesus was leading me as I saw this advertisement: "The Center for Global Education in partnership with Incarnate Word College and Southwestern University is organizing a consciousness raising trip to El Salvador" the coming summer.

In 1981, on my way to Nicaragua, the plane had made a stop in El Salvador. Since that had been seven years earlier, I was interested in a follow up visit. In the interim, Fr. Muccilli and I had made a retreat/workshop in Washington, D.C., focusing on Guatemala at which we learned about conditions there bordering on genocide. After the retreat, we visited with our Congressmen to encourage change in the existing U.S. policy.

2) PILGRIMAGE TO EUROPE.

I led a pilgrimage to Fatima, Rome, Assisi, Florence, Lourdes, Cure of Ars, Paris, the convent of Saint Therese the Little Flower May 29-June 5, 1999.

This pilgrimage began in Portugal with a visit to Fatima where we became participants in a candlelight procession that began in the huge main plaza. On one side of the plaza, we saw the statue of Our Lady of Fatima with the assassin's bullet, that attempted to take the life of John Paul II. We traced the steps of the children of Fatima. We also saw a bit of Lisbon—though not enough.

Our Lady of Fatima, her appearances and messages have profoundly affected many people. What effect does Fatima have on you?

From Fatima we flew to Rome and visited St. Peter's, the Lateran Basilica, the Vatican Museum, Trevi Fountain, the Coliseum, and other sites. Personally, I did not care for Rome. I found staff in the Vatican museum to be quite rude and the traffic was horrendous.

Have you ever had the experience that something everyone raves about, fell short for you or that something that others did not think was so keen, you loved?

From Rome, we took a bus to Assisi, where I could have stayed much longer. I loved the city's atmosphere which appeared to be quite like the time of St. Francis. As I walked the narrow streets, it was easy to imagine scenes from his life.

There are so many aspects to St. Francis of Assisi. For me it was significant that on his election to the papacy, Jorge Mario Bergoglio, the pope of peace, chose the name FRANCIS. It has given inspiration and direction to his ministry: option for the poor, and concern about what we are doing to the earth.

Do you have devotion to Francis, of Assisi and to Pope Francis who came from Argentina?

We then journeyed by bus to Florence where the line to see the famous statue of David was so long that we did not have time to wait. Our visit there was just too short, but then on to Pisa and the Leaning Tower. We moved on along the coast to Monaco and had the opportunity to gamble in a casino. Ours was a daytime visit and we learned that nighttime is much more formal. We spoke about Princess Grace Kelly, the palace and the impressive huge private yachts in the harbor.

By bus, we travelled across to France and on to Lourdes and again participated in a nighttime candle-light procession. The number of sick and disabled people who were incorporated into this procession and praying was very impressive as was the fact that they were cared for so carefully and tenderly. We also participated in a Mass at the grotto, and some of our group ventured into the cold-water baths, I wasn't among them. We saw the train station where people arrive in great numbers to this special place of pilgrimage.

My impression of Lourdes was that, fortunately commercialism has not taken over. There are shops, but the emphasis is on Mary, the sick and miracles. The staff was so impressive in their tender and caring service.

Where I live in the Rio Grande Valley of South Texas, we have a shrine to our Lady of San Juan. Its history is intimately connected with the Shrine in Mexico at San Juan de los Lagos to which I personally had the privilege to lead a pilgrimage which also included a visit to the Basilica of Our Lady of Guadalupe.

The devotion to Our Lady of Guadalupe has spread far and wide. Are you familiar with this story? If not, I urge that you become familiar with it.

Most Catholics have a personal devotion to Mary although some devotions have not received the approbation of Rome (Medjugorje). Do you have a devotion to Mary? Under which of her multiple titles?

Our next stop was at Ars, and the residence of the Cure of Ars. The French priest St. Jean Baptiste Vianney (1786-1859) served as the curé of Ars and worked tirelessly for his people. He was known for his personal holiness and ability to help the troubled. Ars is a humble little village and the church was not very impressive. However, the saint was and still is quite impressive.

We proceeded, heading north, to *Paray Le Monial*, the convent of St. Margaret Mary and the site of the apparitions to her of the Sacred Heart of Jesus. Devotion to the Sacred Heart received great momentum following the revelations to Margaret Mary. However, in 1956, Pope Pius XII wrote and published the Encyclical letter, "On Devotion to the

Sacred Heart of Jesus." This document provided a tectonic shift in the focus of this devotion. I remember probing that letter in great depth during my novitiate experience in 1957.

The next saint we visited was St. Bernadette, in Nevers. Her body is preserved there in a very beautiful convent and church setting.

We then set out for Paris, which was to be the next to the last point on our pilgrimage. Our guide announced that we could stay there until the end of our trip. However, many members of our group had come just because they wanted to visit Lisieux. The guide could not believe that people would prefer Lisieux to Paris, but their energy about this issue convinced her and it was on to Lisieux, where one of the things that impressed me the most were the large photographs of St. Therese's parents displayed on the front of the Basilica. This town had a certain specialness about it that in my mind can only be attributed to the Little Flower.

Clearly, there were different value systems involved. The people of our pilgrimage wanted to visit the town of St. Therese. Our tour guide could not fathom this desire being more important than a couple extra days in Paris.

Has a similar situation been part of your experience, when your value system would make one choice, but others with you would prefer a different option?

For me this journey took me among the communion of Saints, Mary, Francis of Assisi, St. Peter, Cure of Ars, St. Bernadette, St. Margaret Mary, St. Therese of Lisieux and her parents.

My two favorites that I implore are St. Anthony (for lost objects) and my guardian angel.

Who are your favorite Saints? In my life, there are many unnamed saints. Is the same true of you?

3) PILGRIMAGE TO MEXICO. 2002.

In 2002, I organized a pilgrimage to Mexico after speaking with the owner of GO WITH JO tours about my plan. Based on her experience she said, "I don't think you can do it in February." We left on our eight-day pilgrimage on the 3rd day of February following our formidable itinerary: Saltillo, Zacatecas, Fresnillo (Shrine of Santo Nino de Atocha), San Juan de los Lagos, Guanajuato, Mexico City, Queretaro, San Luis Potosi, Matehuala, and Real de Catorce. At our last stop of this trip, we woke up to snow which some of our pilgrims and friends from the Rio Grande Valley had never seen. Our driver altered the final leg of the return trip to take safer roads back and avoid the snow.

Sad to say, Mexico has become a difficult place to travel because of the country's lawlessness. However, we were able to see and contrast Mexico, our southern neighbor and the U.S. In Mexico, each city was different in significant ways. They seemed to have different food, art, music, sometimes slightly different Spanish accents, architecture, and types of agriculture. The U.S. is much more standardized.

We covered many differences of geology, different forms of popular religion and the worshiping style of different places. Clothing varied from the most recent fashions to Indigenous ponchos and sandals. Cathedrals though sharing some similar architectural styles, were personalized in some way.

Have you had similar experience of U.S. cities? Do you have any experience outside of the U.S.? Would you like to?

In this chapter, and the previous one I have focused from 1976 through 2002 on six journeys and spiritual activities that span 26 years of my life. In 1976, I was 38 and in 2002, I was 63. As I write this, I am now 81. I hope these experiences have helped me to grow in wisdom, age and grace before God, women, men and children.

Chapter Eight

Additional Education from Travel, Music, and Art.

WHILE REFLECTING ON EDUCATION I have derived from my journeys, I realized that travel is part of my family DNA. My grandfather's travel business and agency in Liverpool, England was sunk when a German submarine torpedoed a cargo ship on which he carried the insurance. Ever resourceful, in 1928 when my father was fifteen, he brought his six unmarried children to Chicago where his ambition was to convince banks to include a travel agency in their business. He got no takers. Earlier history of my family included moving from Denmark to England in 1856.

It would be difficult to summarize what education I have gained from travel. However, at this point of my life I would like to offer some reflections, especially regarding many stereotypes that have been shattered.

1) Visit to Israel, 1976.

This visit got me in contact with my DNA, which showed I am at least 48% Ashkenazi Jewish. My two cousins in England have vied with each other to shed light on that aspect of our Family tree. From their research, I learned that my great grandfather, who was born in 1823 and died in 1901, was, as the family tree identifies: "Joseph Isackson, later Jackson". He emigrated from Denmark to England, at a time that, evidently, it was better not to have a clearly identifiable Jewish name. This real discrimination so affected my father that he did not share his Jewish heritage with me until I was preparing in 1976 for my study tour to Israel.

The discrimination I witnessed in the treatment of Arabs crossing the Allenby Bridge, from Jordan to Israel, alarmed me. The State of Israel has separated and detached from Religious Judaism (with its several different branches). Clearly now I make a distinction between the Israel of the Bible, the Jewish religion, and the State of Israel. I find much to be critical of in the present State of Israel.

2) South and Central America.

The Spanish and Portuguese came as *Conquistadores*, conquerors, not just as explorers and missionaries. They destroyed the societies of the Incas, Mayas, and Aztecs (viewing them as barbarians and sometimes animals) in the name of Catholicism and the pursuit of gold and silver. I remember how Benedict XVI on a visit to Brazil created a firestorm when he lauded what the Europeans had brought to that country. The religions of the indigenous people of South America, Mexico and the U.S. have so much to teach us, especially as they see the earth from a very different and important perspective. Earth as *Pachamama*, is sacred and to be diligently cared for.

Allow me at this point to make some random thoughts on the Catholic Church in Cusco, Peru. My most recent visit acquainted me with the present sad reality of the Catholic Church. The Cathedral is in the main plaza and it is not cheap to get a ticket to tour, a reality that should have been a warning to me. Inside the several related buildings there is so much gold and a bit of silver, and I learned that the Church owns much of the property around the plaza, which is the magnet for tourists. The shadow side is that the rent the Church charges to the surrounding merchants is exorbitant. Our guide left the Catholic Church in his 20's because of its neglect of the poor.

There is no way to say this without offending: At the second Vatican Council, a small group of bishops made "An option for the Poor". In South America the bishops, at a meeting in Medellin, Colombia, fleshed out its meaning for the countries that they represented. In many places that option continues. However, the institutional Church has consistently resisted this orientation which continues to the present. This reality, however, is not limited to the Southern Hemisphere. In the United States, I believe that much of the resistance to Pope Francis' call for the Church to be a Field Hospital is resisted because bishops and priests are living too comfortably.

A bit of stream of consciousness contributing to the shattering of stereotypes: Cardinal Arns in San Paulo Brazil; Helder Camera in Recife; Liberation Theology: Gustavo Gutierrez and Leonardo Boff; Basic Christian Communities: in Cuernavaca and many other locations. Bishop Sergio Mendez Arceo ("I received a doctorate in Church history, but I was to make history, not teach it"), a supporter of Basic Christian Communities; in Nicaragua Fernando Cardenal and literacy campaign; Fr. Miguel D'Escoto (served in the Sandinista Government but also the founder of Orbis Books). El Salvador: Saint Oscar Romero, Rutilio Grande, Jon Sobrino, SJ. December 2, 1980, five members of the El Salvador National Guard raped and murdered four Catholic missionaries from the United States who were working in El Salvador. They were Maryknoll Sisters Maura Clarke and Ita Ford, Ursuline Dorothy Kazel, and lay missionary Jean Donovan. I remember attending a memorial service at St. Patrick's Catholic Church in downtown Chicago. When we sang "Be Not Afraid" tears overcame my singing as thoughts rushed into my head of the possibility that this could happen to my dear friend, an Ursuline Sister from Kentucky ministering in Callao, Peru.

3) European architecture

It would be difficult to exaggerate the difference between architecture in Europe and in the U.S. It became clear to me that many edifices in Europe took many years to build but were built to last. We tear down so much of our architecture, as the song says, "to build a parking lot". In the U.S., we build, demolish, and build again, in a vicious cycle. An artist friend once alerted me to the reality that "we fashion buildings and then buildings fashion us". The contrast in terms of beauty, form and fashion, and endurance has come alive for me in dramatic fashion by visiting other countries.

4) Music.

Perhaps a little story will illustrate an aspect of music in my life. I like a variety, but liturgical music has a special place in my heart. Some years ago, I was visiting a Catholic parish in Corpus Christi, whose very good music allowed me to sing my heart out. After the Mass, a woman in the pew in front of me turned to me and said, "Are you Protestant?" It continues to remind me that liturgical music and singing in most Catholic Churches can't compare to most Protestant denominations.

However, that of the St. Louis Jesuits, together and in their individual compositions, speaks powerfully to me. I like the Gelineau Psalms. The music of Taize speaks to me. Leonard Cohen's "Halleluia" accompanied me on my daily bike ride for many days after I heard it and sought out the lyrics. Andean music too taps into something in me. Once when I was heartily singing the responsorial, "Be with Me Lord when I am in trouble, be with Me Lord I pray," the words changed to "I'm with you David when you are in trouble, I'm with you David today".

5) ART.

A whole world of art opened for me when I put JESUS THE GAR-DENER into a Google search and I was introduced to the expansive collection portraying Jesus as a Gardener. From this collection comes the Albrecht Dürer (German, 1471–1528),*Noli me tangere, 1511.* a woodcut displayed in London's British Museum which I considered for part of the cover design. Photography is a hobby of mine from which I have learned the power and prayerfulness that images contain. Consequently, I have taken up the practice of collecting works of art that appear in posts on Facebook.

Chapter Nine

My Reading Life.

Books give
a **soul** to the universe,
wings to the mind,
flight to the
imagination,
and **life** to everything.

\- PLATO

My reading life has been a significant element in how I perceive that "Jesus gardens me."

In my bookshelves, I have organized my volumes into several different categories:

1. Scripture.
2. The Historical Jesus.
3. The Passion of Jesus.
4. Social–Science Commentaries.
5. Social teaching of the Catholic Church.
6. Liberation Theology.
7. Tools for understanding personality: Myers-Briggs and Ennea-gram.
8. Sexuality, Feminism, Spirituality of the Sacred Heart, Prayer Styles.
9. Pope Francis.
10. Biographies.
11. Documents of Vatican II.
12. Atlases, Dictionaries, Concordances, and Bibles.

Although many different books in all these categories enriched me, I do have my favorites.

1) **Scripture**: My focus has been on the Gospels. I have a favorite commentary for three of the four: Mark by Ched Myers, Matthew by Warren Carter, John by Wes Howard-Brook. I am eagerly waiting for a commentary on Luke in the same mode.

2) **Historical Jesus**: Somewhere in my ongoing observing, gathering and ruminating (characteristic of those who are Fives on the Enneagram), I came upon Jose A. Pagola and his meditations on the Gospels of each cycle. Although I have a whole shelf of books on Jesus, the tentativeness of one of his titles, *Jesus: An Historical Approximation*, fascinated me. The accompanying blurb further drew me in, noting, "Pagola reconstructs the complete historical figure of Jesus with scholarly,

exegetical, and theological approach, in an easy to read language." In the last chapter, "Exploring the Identity of Jesus," he offers brief information about the four Gospels, then moves on to a section called "Find the right Name for Jesus," in which he considers each of the titles Messiah, A New Man, High Priest, Lord, Incarnate Word of God and Son of God.

I have become more and more committed to exploring the Human Jesus. One summary of Mark refers to him as "The hurried, harried, Human Jesus". Ever since my M.A. studies at Catholic Theological Union, I have studied, preached, and taught courses on this Gospel. Fr. Don Senior, on the faculty, taught an entire course on Mark's Gospel. It got me hooked.

There have been too many accretions put on Jesus that have strayed from the original, and in the first two chapters of this book, I have presented my case for this observation. I have also come to a changed understanding of who Jesus was and his mission. I truly believe, that with Constantine, the Church was compromised. Now it was being formed by the state rather than informing the state. This new understanding of Jesus has led me, in the last year or so, to identify myself this way: "I no longer call myself a Catholic, but rather I am a follower of Jesus". It has a positive resonance for me, and I am finding others also find it so.

3) **The Passion of Jesus:** Two U.S. scholars, experts on this subject, are Raymond Brown and Donald Senior. I have studied their work and have taught courses on the Passion. Brown wrote a popular treatment of the Passion narratives before publishing his scholarly two-volume work. In this popular version, he stated, "My hope in writing on . . . the passion narratives has been to supply ample material for reflection on both sides of the pulpit and to show that contemporary critical biblical research can be pastorally serviceable".**65** Not all Scripture scholars have this ability. My list of those who do includes Eugene LaVerdiere, Carol Stuhlmueller, Barbara Reid, and Diane Bergant.

4) **Social–Science Commentaries**: The influence and impact of this area of study has changed my ideas about the conditions in which

Jesus lived and worked. Two works by Douglas Oakman have impacted my understanding of Jesus and the theory I have proposed about his occupation.

5) **Social teaching of the Catholic Church**: For fifty years, I was a member of the Priests of the Sacred Heart. The founder of this Congregation was Father Leo John Dehon. who was involved in promulgating and applying the message of Leo XIII's Encyclical, *Rerum Novarum.* This encyclical is the first, in modern times, of many Papal teachings on the Social Doctrine of the Catholic Church. During my years with the Priests of the Sacred Heart, various members involved in social justice issues influenced and inspired me.

6) **Liberation Theology**: A turning point in my life happened in 1981, the experience I've described in Chapter 6. In preparation for my consciousness-raising trip, I read *A Theology of Liberation* by Gustavo Gutierrez. This highly informative book helped prepare me for my actual experiences which spoke even more powerfully.

7) **Tools for understanding personality**: I am not sure when I first encountered the Myers-Briggs Type Indicator and the Enneagram. What I am sure of is that these two personality tools have helped me to self-discovery, deeper spirituality and a fuller prayer life.

8) **Sexuality, Feminism, and Spirituality of the Sacred Heart**: Perhaps encountering this combination in my listing may seem strange. Without trying to explain the combination, I will simply note books under the separate categories.

Sexuality: *Just Love* (A Framework for Christian Spiritual Ethics) by Margaret A. Farley; *Human Sexuality A Study Commissioned by the Catholic Theological Society of America; Between Two Gardens (Reflection on Sexuality and Religious Experience)* by James B. Nelson.

Feminism: *Women's Reality* by Anne Wilson Schaff; *Diving Deep and Surfacing* by Carol P. Christ, *The Feminist Mystic* edited by Mary E.

Giles; *In a Different Voice* by Carol Gilligan; *Beyond Anger* by Carolyn Osiek, RSCJ, *Women Who Run with the Wolves* by Clarissa Pinkola Estes, Ph.D.

Spirituality of the Sacred Heart: *Heart of the Savior* by R. Gutzwiller, H. Rahner, K. Rahner and J. Stierli with the Encyclical *Haurietis Aquas* by Pope Pius XII.

9) **Pope Francis.** One of my considered blessings in these advanced years of my life has been the election of Pope Francis. His demeanor, his homilies, his discourses, his interviews, and press conferences in flight have spoken powerfully to me. As far as my reading life, here is an incomplete list: his Apostolic Exhortations, Encyclical, and *The Name of God is Mercy*, Books about Pope Francis: *The Great Reformer* by Austen Ivereigh, *Life and Revolution FRANCIS*, by Elisabetta Pique. Subsequently I came *upon PILGRIMAGE (My Search for the Real Pope Francis)* by Mark K. Shriver. Biographer Austen Ivereigh captures my estimation of the book: "Funny, wise, insightful, and skillfully penned, *Pilgrimage* deserves to be ranked among the best books on the greatest leader of our age."

10) **Biographies.**

Thomas Merton, a Trappist priest whose biography is intriguing with its twists and turns. Pope Francis when he spoke to the U.S. Congress, September 24, 2015, summed up why Merton is important to me:

A century ago, at the beginning of the Great War, which Pope Benedict XV termed a "pointless slaughter", another notable American was born: the Cistercian monk Thomas Merton. He remains a source of spiritual inspiration and a guide for many people. In his autobiography he wrote: "I came into the world. Free by nature, in the image of God, I was nevertheless the prisoner of my own violence and my own selfishness, in the image of the world into which I was born. That world was the picture of Hell, full of men like myself loving God, and yet hating him; born to love him, living instead in fear of hopeless self-contradictory hungers". Merton was above all a man of prayer, a thinker who challenged the certitudes of his time and opened new horizons for souls and for the Church. He was also a man of dialogue, a promoter of peace between peoples and religions.

Pierre Teihlhard de Chardin, SJ, was a French philosopher and Jesuit priest, trained as a paleontologist and geologist. Though his writings were not allowed to be published in his lifetime, after his death they were published and inspired many people, including me.

John Fitzgerald Kennedy inspired many people by his writings, speeches and assassination. His death was a heavy blow to me. I was among those who watched the entire broadcast of his funeral.

Mohandas Karamchand Gandi. His life was marked most profoundly by his stance of non-violence. It also ended with assassination,

Martin Luther King, Jr. was among those inspired by the actions and writings of Gandi. and was assassinated.

Archbishop Rembert Weakland. He had a wide-ranging experience of the world as the head of the Benedictines. His career ended abruptly when it became public that he had paid a man not to expose his homosexual relationship. He was an excellent preacher and, accomplished musician. The homily he gave at the Holy Saturday liturgy inspired me so much that I preached it at many Holy Saturday vigils.

Cardinal Donald Wuerl. He was tapped by the Vatican to investigate Archbishop Hunthausen. His skillful handling of that assignment brought him to the attention of the Vatican. His career as bishop in different dioceses and finally the Archdiocese of Washington, D.C. was noted for his balance. But his handling of a priest accused of sexual misconduct, led to his forced retirement.

Daniel Berrigan,SJ. Though most known for his protests and arrests, he was also a poet, student of Scripture and writer of Commentaries on Books of the Bible.

11) **Documents of Vatican II.** During the sessions of the Second Vatican Council I was a teacher at a high school seminary in Lenox, Massachusetts. I found out that the Davenport Register was publishing the Documents as they were approved by those Bishops in attendance.

I avidly read them and was inspired especially by the Documents on Liturgy, Divine Revelation, The Church in the Modern World and those dealing with Ecumenism.

12) Atlases, Dictionaries, Concordances and Bibles.

SECTION THREE:

Further Application For Life.

Chapter Ten

May Jesus Garden You.

Pope Francis' first publication as Pope—written in the clear understandable language for which he is known-- was "The Joy of the Gospel" in which the first sentence proclaims his top priority: "The Joy of the Gospel fills the hearts and lives of all who encounter Jesus"**66**. In the second paragraph he warns that the "The great danger in today's world, pervaded as it is by consumerism, is the desolation and anguish born of complacent yet covetous heart, the feverish pursuit of frivolous pleasures, and a blunted conscience," noting that "Many . . . end up resentful, angry, and listless"**67**. But he offers an antidote: "I invite all Christians, everywhere, at this very moment, to a renewed personal encounter with Jesus Christ, or at least an openness to letting him encounter them; I ask all of you to do this unfailingly each day."**68** The rest of this Apostolic Exhortation presents a detailed program for the Church. It is written in the famous style of the pope--plain everyday language.

For me, his message is a touching reminder that the meeting of Mary Magdalene in the Garden with Jesus was the culmination of a friendship, which must have developed over some time. We do not know much from scripture about this friendship and what we have is scanty. However, it surely was a process.

I have found St. Teresa of Avila, too, to write in everyday language when considering the stages of prayer. She describes, in her autobiography, a process for us to ponder in building a "renewed encounter with Jesus Christ". I discovered that a 24-year-old anonymous blogger, summarized this process:

For St. Teresa, the purpose of life is union with God. This is likewise the purpose of prayer. Therefore, the purpose of life is union with God through prayer. In her discussion, she uses the metaphor of a garden, the earth being the soul and the water being the understanding of Grace. She says, "A beginner must look on himself as one setting out to make a garden for His Lord's pleasure, on most unfruitful soil which abounds in weeds. His Majesty roots up the weeds and will put in good plants instead."

Saint Teresa explains in considerable detail the progressive journey of prayer by using the symbol of four methods of watering a garden.

The first method draws water from a well by means of a bucket attached to a rope, a process in which there is quite a bit of hard work and not a great quantity of water is captured.

The second method uses a water wheel to which dippers are attached. As the wheel is turned, the water is poured into a trough that carries it to the garden. This procedure needs less work and produces a greater quantity of water.

Then there is irrigation by means of a running stream, which does not call for human effort as in the two previous methods. Prayer at this stage is mystical; that is, all the faculties are centered on God.

Finally, a garden is watered by means of falling rain, reflecting the stage of prayer that is totally mystical, as it is infused by God and is not attained by human effort. It is called the prayer of union and it admits varying degrees.**69**

Where am I in the process of union with God through prayer? How is the gardener leading me? What are things that help me to advance in prayer? What do I need in order to advance?

SAKKIEH, OR WATER-WHEEL.

Postscript

ON THE WEBSITE "CATHOLIC WOMEN Preach" for July 16, 2017, noted theologian Erin Lothes gives us much to ponder in the lectionary readings for the 15th Sunday of Cycle A. I found this piece to connect with my own title for this book, JESUS GARDENS ME. It also calls attention to what is happening in the "garden of the World" and our own responsibility in the wake of the ecological crisis. My focus has been on my experience of Jesus Gardening me. This post highlights the call to all of us to take on the task of being Gardeners for the world we now live in. In her words: "This is the labor God has called us to as fellow gardeners." (I thank the author for permission to publish this post.)

Summertime in the glorious outdoors . . . a time to savor the joy and relaxation of summer Sabbath, the season of vacation and re-creation.

The gifts of Sabbath alternate with our seasons of work-- the rest and gratitude that renews us for our labors.

Are we ready to rest, confident we have been caring for the garden? This earth is so beautiful and fruitful, and yet the impacts of climate change are felt in many places around the world, where heat, drought, storm impacts, coastal erosion, and loss of biodiversity are affecting the poor first and worst.

We are called not only to care for our jobs and our families, but to protect the garden of our common home, the earth we all share.

The doctrine of creation in the Catechism teaches that God has given us the responsibility, the freedom and the dignity, to be God's workers in the garden of this world.

What an audacious risk God has taken! But as we see the environmental damage in so many places, creation seems truly subject to futility from human carelessness.

What if, as the poet Mary Oliver says, God's plan was that we would do better?

At times our weary hearts are like hardened soil, overwhelmed by the news of environmental damage, and ceasing to hear the cry for action. Our busy lives are like soil without depth, without the time or energy to make real changes for sustainable communities.

We all have many cares and serious obligations: our jobs, families, legitimate demands for our time. But take an honest look into the weeds. Are there thorny distractions and trivial pursuits preventing us from changing unsustainable habits? We need to make time for this, addressing what Pope Francis calls a complex environmental and social crisis. Because the poor suffer worst and the beauty of God's creation is dimmed, *Laudato Si* teaches that this work is "neither optional nor secondary." As Saint Pope John Paul II wrote twenty-five years ago, "The ecological crisis has reached such proportions as to be the moral responsibility of everyone."

How can the word accomplish the renewal God intends in our time of climate change?

The parable of the sower teaches that the word of God does not bloom in mid-air. The word of God is not a hydroponic tomato! It is not accomplished by God's unilateral action. The word of God must take root in our lives, in the soil of our hearts, because God has pitched his tent among us, and entrusted Creation to our labor.

The psalmist praises God for the seed that will yield a fruitful harvest as God prepares the land, softening it with showers. Our hearts are likewise refreshed by the hopeful word of God's eternal will to be Creator. And Isaiah promises that God's will shall be accomplished. In Jesus, God's word is the good news of forgiveness, healing, abundance, an overflowing wedding feast -- the return of the lost and the welcome of all refugees at God's table, the redemption of creation groaning in labor pains.

Has God the Creator once again accepted the possibilities of chaos?

In the beginning the Spirit of God moved upon the chaos to create. Could it be that the chaos of now is open to a new time of creativity and renewal?

Renewal comes as our listening hearts accept the pain of hearing the reality of those now suffering the impacts of climate change. Can we allow this heartbreak to be a means of conversion, of turning over the soil? Here is where we roll up our sleeves and get our hands dirty. Pull out those thorns of a lesser priority. Make time for one, then another, transforming commitment to the earth in your life.

Give depth to your green wishes-- we can do more than a lightbulb, a coffee cup, a canvas bag. Pope Francis calls for a bold cultural revolution that is in fact a very traditional re-covery-- recovering the values of conservation, of frugality, of stewardship, of reverent care for the beautiful earth. These are deeply conservative values which appear radical in our time. And it is this new depth we must bring to the shallow soil. We can choose actions with real impact: to buy clean wind and solar energy through our utilities, to reduce the waste of food and disposables and excess driving. We can support clean energy jobs, efficiency, energy security and cleaner air and water, ending the pollution that harms the stability of earth's sacred order.

We can voice and vote our values, calling for clean energy solutions for our communities and we can pray and rejoice in our churches for the gifts of God's beautiful Creation, whose garden brings forth gifts for the sustenance of all.

This is the labor God has called us to as fellow gardeners.

For we have no right to contribute to the degradation of God's earth.

And although earth now bears the thorny crown of the suffering of the poor and struggling ecosystems, we know all Creation will be redeemed in God's holy plan for creation and salvation. Amidst the chaos God's spirit pours out in our hearts, so that they will be renewed through God's fruitful word, knowing that all will see the glory of God's Creation,

And all, in our day, may join in the abundant banquet God intends.

Then our summer Sabbath will truly be a blessed time of rest amidst our labors for our common home.

Notes

1. Johnson, Still believe in Miracles, 14.
2. Jones, Mistook for gardener. April 5, 2016,
3. Audlin, No Mistake.
4. Meier, Marginal Jew, 279.
5. Meier, Marginal, 312, footnote, 165.
6. Malina, Rohrbaugh, . Social-Science Commentary on the Synoptic Gospels 175.
7. Kelber, Mark's Story 1979.
8. Hanson, Oakman, Palestine Time of Jesus, 10.
9. Jones, Mistook for gardener. April 5, 2016.
10. Brown, Birth of Messiah, appendix.
11. Donaldson. Infancy Gospel of Thomas #12.
12. Oakman, 1986, 179.
13. Furfey, "Christ as Tekton"324-335, 1955.
14. Meier, Marginal Jew, 278-285.
15. Tabor, Republished post from December 28, 2017 titled Was Jesus a Carpenter.
16. Donahue, Gospel in Parable, ix.
17. Borg, Meeting Jesus Again for the First Time, 26.
18. Crossan, Jesus: A Revolutionary Biography, 24.
19. Pilch, The Bible Today, January 1994.
20. Oakman,1986, 179.

21. Pilch, Bible Today.

22. Pagola, Jesus An Historical Approximation, 47.

23. Oakman, Jesus and the Economic Questions of his day, 180.

24. Oakman, 182.

25. Oakman, 187.

26. Oakman, 178.

27. Oakman, Jesus and the Peasants, 171.

28. Meier, Marginal Jew, 312, footnote, 165 112.

29. Oakman, Jesus and the Economic Questions of his Day, 193.

30. Oakman, Jesus and the Peasants, 38.

31. Oakman, 296-297.

32. Oakman, 2008, 308.

33. Howard-Brook, Empire Baptized (How the Church Embraced What Jesus Rejected 2nd-5th Centuries.

34. Oakman, 2008, 172.

35. Oakman, 296, 297.

36. Jones, Mistook for gardener. April 5, 2016.

37. Mullen, Sermon, July 22, 2018.

38. Audlin, No Mistake.

39. Schneiders, Written That You May Believe, 197-198.

40. Titian, Noli Me Tangere.

41. Mullen, Jesus the Gardener.

42. Veritas, Jesus the Gardener.

43. Howard-Brook, Becoming Children of God, 449.

44. Schineller, blog: Jesus the Gardener.

45. Nelson Between Two Gardens, 7-8.

46. Times Magazine, June 20, 1988.

47. Haskins, Mary Magdalen.

48. Brant, John, 269.

49. Jones, Sewing the Stigmata.

50. Titian, Noli me Tangere.

51. Jones, She Mistook Him for the Gardener.

52. Mullen, Jesus the Gardener.

53. This entry was posted in Hudgins (Andrew) and tagged "Ascension"," Christ the Gardener".

54. Howard-Brook, Becoming Children of God, 447.

55. Donaghy, Walk the Way.

56. Jones, She Mistook Him for the Gardener.

57. Donohue, Congregational Experience.

58. Kramer-Rolls, Jesus the Gardener.

59. Hall, Jesus the Gardener.

60. Rohr, Jesus of Nazareth, January 20, 2018.

61. Rohr, Jesus of Nazareth, January 20, 2018.

62. Johnson, Still believe in Miracles. 14.

63. Rohr, Jesus of Nazareth, January 20, 2018.

64. Bailey, Jesus Through Middle Eastern Eyes. 28-36.

65. Brown, Crucified Christ, Foreword.

66. Pope Francis, Evangelii Gaudium, 1.

67. Pope Francis, Evangelii Gaudium, 2.

68. Pope Francis, Evangelii Gaudium, 3.

69. Teresa of Avila, The book of Her Life, chapter. 13.

Bibliography

Audlin, James David. No Mistake: Mary was Right to Think Jesus was the Gardener. ACADEMIA *Gospel of John Restored and Translated,* 2016.

Bailey, Kenneth E. Jesus through Middle Eastern Eyes (Cultural Studies in the Gospels). Downers Grove, Illinois: IPV Academic, 2008.

Barclay, William. Gospel of Mark. Philadelphia: Westminster, 1956.

Beavis, Mary Ann. Mark. Grand Rapids, Michigan: Baker Academic, 2011.

Binz, Stephen J. Passion and RESURRECTION, Narratives of Jesus/A Commentary. Collegeville, Minnesota: Liturgical Press, 1989.

Brant, Jo-Ann A. John. Grand Rapids, Michigan: Baker Academic. 2011.

Brown, Raymond. Birth of the Messiah (Appendix), Yale University Press, Dec. 3, 2007. ___. Crucified Christ in Holy Week. Collegeville, Minnesota: Liturgical Press, 1986.

Borg, Marcus. Jesus: *Uncovering the Life, Teachings, and Relevance of a Religious Revolutionary.* SanFrancisco: Harper, 2006. Borg originally offered these comments on NBC's *Today Show,* Good Friday, 1995.

Capps, Donald. Jesus the Village Psychiatrist. Louisville: Westminster John Knox, 2008.

Crossan, John Dominic. Jesus: A Revolutionary Biography. San Francisco: Harpers, 1994.

Didi-Huberman, Georges (posted by Victoria Emily Jones on the blog *Revitalizing the Christian imagination through painting, poetry, music, and more* Sowing the Stigmata): A reading of Fra Angelico's Noli me tangere, April 20, 2018.

Donaghy, John. Walk the Way "Christ the Gardener" March 31, 2013.
___. Walk the Way "Care for the Garden" April 22, 2014.

Donahue, *Teresa M. CSJP "A Congregational Experience Program: Meeting the Gardener" Sisters Today, April 1988.*

Donaldson, Roberts. Infancy Gospel of Thomas. Early Christian Writings.English Translation: First Greek Form. #12.

Ellis, Peter F. Genius of John (A Composition-Critical Commentary on the Fourth Gospel: Collegeville, Minnesota: Liturgical Press, 1984

Francis, Pope. Apostolic Exhortation, *Evangelii Gaudium, Liberia Editrice Vaticana, Rome,* 11/24/2013.

Freyne, Sean. JESUS A Jewish Galilean (a new reading of the Jesus-story). New York: T & Clark international, 2004.

Furfey, Paul Hanly. "Christ as *Tekton"*Catholic Biblical Quarterly, *Vol 17p324-335, 1955.*

Hall, Dudley. (Posted on blog STEAM) Jesus the Gardener. **March 30, 2018.**

Hanson, K.C. & Oakman, Douglas E. Palestine in the Time of Jesus (Social Structures and Social Conflicts) second edition. Minneapolis, Minnesota: Augsburg Fortress, 2008.

Haskins, Susan. Mary Magdalen (Myth and Metaphor). New York: Harcourt Brace,1994:

Howard-Brook, Wes. Becoming Children of God (John's Gospel and Radical Discipleship). Eugene Oregon: Wipf and Stock, 2003.

Johnson, Luke Timothy. Commonweal, 14-19, February 22, 2019.

Jones, Victoria Emily. On the blog *revitalizing the Christian imagination through painting, poetry, music, and more* She Mistook him for the Gardener, April 5, 2016. ___. Sowing the stigmata: A reading of Fra Angelico's *Noli me tangere* by Georges Didi-Huberman, April 20, 2018.

Kelber, Werner H. Mark's Story of Jesus. Philadelphia: Fortress, 1979.

Kramer-Rolls, Dana. On the blog Episcopal Café, Jesus the Gardener, April 2, 2018.

Malina, Bruce J. and Rohrbaugh. Social-Science Commentary on the Synoptic Gospels. Minneapolis, Minnesota: Augsburg Fortress, 1992. ___. Social-Science Commentary on the Gospel of John. Minneapolis.: Augsburg Fortress, 1998.

Malina, Bruce J. New Testament World (revised edition) Insights from Cultural Anthropology. Louisville, Kentucky: Westminster/John Knox, 1993. ___. Windows on the World of Jesus. (Time Travel to Ancient Judea). Louisville, Kentucky: Westminster/John Knox, 1993.

Meier, John P. Marginal Jew, Rethinking the Historical Jesus. New York: Doubleday, 1991.

Mullen, Fr. Sean. Sermon at St. Mark's Church, Philadelphia. Jesus the Gardener., July 22, 2018.

Myers, Ched. Binding the Strong Man (A Political Reading of Mark's Story of Jesus). Maryknoll, N.Y.: Orbis Books, 1997. ___. "Say to This Mountain" (Mark's Story of Discipleship). Maryknoll, N.Y.: Orbis Books, 1996.

Nelson, James B. Between Two Gardens. New York: Pilgrim Press, 1983.

Oakman, Douglas E. Jesus and the Economic Questions of His Day. Lewiston-Queenston: Edwin Mellen Press, 1986. ___. Jesus and the Peasants. Eugene, Oregon: Cascade Books, 2008.

Pagola, Jose A. Following in the Footsteps of Jesus: (Meditations on the Gospels for Year B). Miami, Florida: Convivium, 2011.

Pilch, John. The Cultural World of Jesus (Cycles A B C). Minnesota: Liturgical, 1996.

Reid, Barbara E. Parables for Preachers, Year A: Collegeville, Minnesota: The Order of St. Benedict, 1999.

Rohr, Fr. Richard. Jesus of Nazareth. Jesus, January 20, 2018. Adapted from Jesus Plan for a new World: The Sermon on the Mount. Franciscan Media: 1996), vii-viii.

Sabin, Marie Noonan. Gospel According to Mark. Minnesota: The Order of St. Benedict, 2006.

Schineller, S.J. blog: Jesus the Gardener. March 31, 2013.

Schneiders, Sandra M. Revelatory Text (Interpreting the New Testament as Sacred Scripture). New York: HarperCollins, 1991. ___. Written that You May Believe (Encountering Jesus in the Fourth Gospel). New York: The Crossroad 1999.

Spurgeon, C.H. Sermon # 1699, Supposing Him to be the Gardener, Metropolitan Tabernacle, Newington, December 31, 1882.

Teresa of Avila. The Book of Her Life. Indianapolis: Hackett Publishing Company, 1995.

Thurston, Bonnie B. The Spiritual Landscape of Mark. Collegeville, Minnesota: The Order of St. Benedict, 2008.

Made in the USA
Coppell, TX
24 May 2020

25892119R00081